MAMMY PLEASANT'S COOKBOOK

Compiled and Edited By
HELEN HOLDREDGE

Illustrated By
JAMES BEAUCHAMP ALEXANDER

101 PRODUCTIONS
San Francisco

TO ALLAN OTTLEY

Supervisor of the California Section
of the California State Library
in appreciation of his unflagging interest
and help with research over the years.

Published by 101 Productions
79 Liberty Street, San Francisco, California
Printed in the United States of America
All Rights Reserved
Standard Book Number 0-912238-04-6

CONTENTS

PUBLISHER'S PREFACE

From Boston to Charlestown to New Orleans to San Francisco, Mary Ellen Pleasant cooked her way to fame, fortune and a fantastic power over some of the most influential citizens of the 19th century. Born a slave and later freed, she learned to cook in New England; then developed her art on Southern Plantations and in the home of the Voodoo Queen of New Orleans. Armed with her culinary talents and an acute business skill, she arrived in San Francisco at the height of its bonanza days. Here she operated several elite boarding houses and served as housekeeper to some of the city's most prominent citizens. As her fame as the most outstanding cook in the West grew, she used her contacts to amass a fortune.

Helen Holdredge, author of the best-selling biography *Mammy Pleasant*, devoted many years to solving the mysteries of the Mammy Pleasant legends, searching for material and interviewing those who had known Mammy in many sections of the United States. During her research she acquired a number of Mammy's recipe books, along with her other papers. The proportions were so large that it was certain that the recipes had been set down for her assistant cooks in her three San Francisco boarding houses.

The recipes, however, were fascinating. For wherever Mammy Pleasant lived she learned the regional cooking and then added her own exotic touches. Because she lived in the areas where the cuisine was the most colorful, Mammy's cookbooks become an anthology of the regional gourmet cookery of 19th century America.

Over a period of years, Mrs. Holdredge, an accomplished cook in her own right, tested the recipes and equated them to smaller amounts, in some cases adding ingredients unknown to the cooks of that period.

"Some of the recipes could not be included because of the impossibility of finding certain ingredients," Mrs. Holdredge admits. "For instance the inclusion of 'three pounds of crumps' in a recipe for Spanish cookies, the use of 'molasses drops' in Mondel bread are as puzzling as Mac Landas, surely the name of a person, written above what turned out to be the least understandable recipe of all: 3/4 quart sugar, 1/2 pound butter, 1 pound flour, 8 yolks of eggs, 1/2 ounce amm."

MAMMY PLEASANT

Mary Ellen Pleasants, who was later to become famous as Mammy Pleasant, was born a slave on a plantation near Augusta, Georgia. A quadroon of very light coloring, with one blue eye and one brown, she had an extremely brilliant mind. It was this quality that attracted the attention of a wealthy planter, Americus Price of Price's Landing, Missouri. He purchased the nine year old girl and sent her to the Ursaline convent in New Orleans to be educated. She assimilated a great deal in the year she was there and Price decided this amazing girl should not remain in slave-holding territory. After a time in Cincinnati she was finally sent to Nantucket Island to a Quakeress named Mrs. Mary Hussey, the owner of a dry goods store on Union Street, "Under the Hill."

NANTUCKET

COOKERY

NANTUCKET COOKERY

From 1824 to 1839 Mary Ellen worked in Mrs. Hussey's and learned the island ways. After the first frost of autumn she gathered bayberries to make holiday candles, made jelly from wild beach plums and learned to cook the dishes served during the island's prosperous whaling days.

Her stove was an open fireplace with a huge pot hanging from a crane and several other pots sat on trivets. The skillets and spiders (or three-legged frying pans) she used were greased with suet or butter tied in a rag. A slender pointed rod was used to hold meats over the fire. Her oven was called a "kitchen" and it was made of deep plates of block tin, surrounded by hot coals when baking was to be done. Her "paste-board" was a marble slab. Loaf sugar had to be powdered. Mace came in blades, nutmegs were whole and cinnamon bark came only in stick form. The onions used in stuffings were parboiled. Baking powder was little used and was referred to as sal-aratus. Roasts were tied with packet thread.

Grandma Hussey's Store on Nantucket Island

OYSTER SOUP

Use 1 quart of oysters and parboil for 15 minutes. Strain the water off the oysters and put them in 1 quart of beef stock. Add 1/2 cup of white sauce to which has been added a teaspoonful of Worcestershire sauce, 1 tablespoonful of minced parsley, a bay leaf and 1 whole clove. Stir into the beef stock, add 1 cup of heavy cream. Bring slowly to a boil, remove bay leaf and clove and serve.

BASIC RECIPE FOR WHITE SAUCE

Melt 6 tablespoonsful of butter in an iron frying pan. Remove from heat. Blend into the melted butter 8 tablespoonsful of flour until the paste is absolutely smooth. Then add 2/3 cup of water. Gradually stir in 1 cup of milk over low heat and add 1/4 teaspoonful of salt. Stir for at least four minutes. If the sauce grows too thick a little more milk may be added.

NANTUCKET CHOWDER

Cut 1 pound of fresh haddock or fresh cod into medium sized pieces. Slowly fry 2 slices of thickly cut bacon. Remove bacon from pan when done and then slowly fry 1 onion, which has been sliced, in the bacon fat. When lightly brown, remove to a dish. Next thinly slice 3 potatoes. Into a kettle place layers of fish and layers of potatoes. Cover with water and simmer over low heat. Meantime prepare a white sauce by slowly melting over lowest heat 4 tablespoonsful of butter. Remove from heat and stir in 5 tablespoonsful of flour and stir until smooth. Add 1/2 cup water and make a smooth paste. Return to heat adding milk, a little at a time, until the sauce thickens into a heavy creaminess and remove from heat. Dice the already fried bacon and add to the onions. Stir into the sauce, then add 1 sliced hard boiled egg, 1/4 teaspoonful of pepper, and 1/4 teaspoonful of marjoram. When the simmered potatoes and fish are done drain and place sauce over them.

NANTUCKET COOKERY

MRS. HUSSEY'S SALT CODFISH

Soak 2 pounds of dried codfish in cold water for twelve hours with two changes of water. Put into boiling water and when the water has again come to a boil reduce the heat to simmering stage and cook for six hours.

SOUR CREAM SAUCE FOR CODFISH

Cook 4 green onions, chopped fine, in 2 tablespoonsful of oil (olive oil is best). Add 1 tablespoonful of minced parsley, 1/4 teaspoonful of marjoram, 1/4 teaspoonful of sweet basil, 1 tablespoonful of mustard (prepared), salt and pepper to taste and a cup of sour cream. Pour over fish and heat under a flame.

"UNDER THE HILL" SOLE

Select firm fillets of sole. Soak first in very cold milk. Lift out and dip in flour. Fry the fillets in hot fat until crisp and nicely brown. Quickly drain. Have already prepared a sauce made by blending 4 tablespoonsful softened butter with 1 tablespoonful of Worcestershire sauce, 1/4 teaspoonful of marjoram and 1/4 teaspoonful of lemon juice. Spread sauce over fish and garnish with parsley.

NASTURTIUM SEEDS USED AS GARNISH

Select small green nasturtium seeds. Pickle in salt water for one week, changing the water twice. Then cover the seeds with hot vinegar with a small amount of alum in it.

NANTUCKET COOKERY

VEAL BROTH WITH MARROW BALLS

Use 2 pounds of veal joint and put in stewpan 3/4 full of cold water. Let come to a boil and then simmer until the meat is tender, having added right at first celery leaves, 3 black peppers, an onion and 1 carrot. After meat is done strain soup slowly into saucepan which contains 2 heaping tablespoonsful of flour and 2 tablespoonsful of melted butter which has been well blended. After all liquid has been added bring to a boil, then stir over less heat for 2 or 3 minutes.

MARROW BALLS

Remove marrow from soup bone. Carefully melt over low heat. Strain the melted fat through cheese cloth, beat until creamy and add a well beaten egg.

Season with salt, pepper and a very small amount of marjoram. Add 1/2 cup of bread crumbs to the mixture and form into little balls. Poach these in a small amount of salted boiling water, turning them over to evenly cook, then add to the soup.

INDIAN PUDDING

Heat four cups of milk and add 2/3 cup of molasses, 1/3 cup of granulated sugar, and 1/2 cup of yellow cornmeal. Stir in 3/4 teaspoonful of cinnamon, 3/8 teaspoonful of nutmeg, 1 teaspoonful of salt and 4 tablespoonsful of butter. Cook over low heat until mixture begins to thicken. Pour into the mixture one cup of cold milk and then pour into a baking dish. Arrange on the top slices of pears. Bake for 3 hours until a knife comes out clean when thrust into the pudding. (350°.)

NANTUCKET COOKERY

BLUEBERRY GRUNT

To 2 cups of blueberries, washed and well drained, add 1/2 cup of sugar and 1 cup of water. Mix and sift into mixture 1 cup of flour, 2 teaspoonsful of baking powder and 1/4 teaspoonful of salt. Add 1/2 cup of milk. The dumpling dough is then dropped by spoonfuls into boiling water. Cook for 10 minutes with the cover off and 10 minutes with the cover on. Serve with sweetened whipped cream lightly flavored with nutmeg.

HUCKLEBERRY PUDDING

To 1 cup of shortening add 2 cups of sugar and blend well. Then add the yolks of five eggs. Sift into mixture alternately with 1 cup of milk, 3 cups of flour mixed with 1 teaspoonful of cinnamon and 1 teaspoonful of nutmeg. Dissolve 1 teaspoonful of baking soda in a small amount of hot water. Add to mixture. Then fold in the stiffly beaten whites of the 5 eggs. At last stir in carefully 4 cups of huckleberries that have been thoroughly drained and then dredged with flour. Bake (at 350°) in a cake pan lined with greased paper. When a straw thrust through the center of the pudding comes out clean the pudding is done.

BLACKBERRY WINE

Wash 2 gallons of berries and add 4 quarts of boiling water. Let stand for 12 hours. Strain, pressing the pulp until only the hard sections remain. Measure the liquid and for each gallon of liquid add 2 cups of brown sugar. Put mixture into either a wooden cask or a pottery jug with the cork loosely inserted. Fermentation takes place in about ten days. Then the wine may be sealed up and put away in a dark place for future use.

ELDERBERRY WINE

Pour 4 quarts of boiling water over 3 gallons of elderberries. Strain through cheesecloth mashing the berries until all juice has been extracted. Measure the amount of liquid. Add 3 pounds of sugar, 1/2 ounce of ground ginger, 6 whole cloves and 1 pound of raisins to every 4 gallons. Boil for 1 hour, skimming off any scum which rises to the surface. Then let cool until liquid is just warm. Next add 1/4 pint of brandy to each gallon of liquid and 1 yeast cake to every 4 gallons of liquid. Set aside for two weeks to ferment. Then the wine can be bottled and sealed but not used for at least three months.

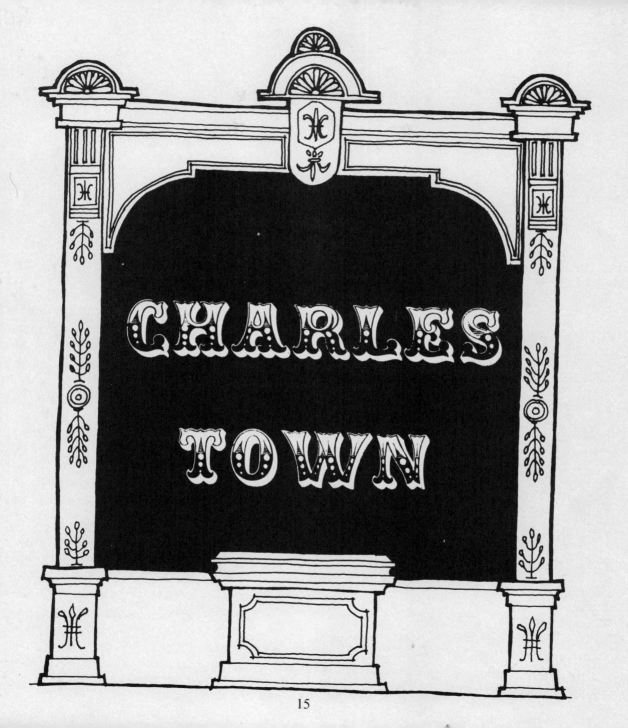

CHARLES TOWN

Smith's Plantation in Charlestown West Virginia

CHARLESTOWN

After the ancient Hussey store, black with age, was destroyed by fire the elderly Quakeress passed away. Mary Ellen managed to find her way to Boston and there met and married a wealthy Cuban planter, James Smith. In addition to his tobacco plantation at Charles Town he owned a home in Boston where he had a contracting business.

During those times at the plantation Mary Ellen learned much about the making of cheeses and the smoking of meats and had both pork and mutton available.

CHARLESTOWN

PLANTATION LAMB

Remove the bone from a 5 pound leg of lamb and then prepare the dressing. Melt 2 tablespoonsful of butter and brown in it 1 small minced onion. To 4 cups of broken-up stale bread add 1/4 teaspoonful each sage and ground cloves, salt and pepper. Add melted butter and onions and mix well. Add 1 cup of halved, cooked apricots. Moisten the whole with apricot juice. Place the dressing inside the lamb and tie into a roll with packet thread. Lay over the roast several pieces of thickly sliced bacon. Bake at 400° for 1/4 hour and then lower heat to 350° and bake another 20 minutes to the pound.

PIG-PORK IN CORN HUSK

Cut a pork shoulder into 10 steaks. Remove the bones and shake salt and pepper on meat. Prepare a stuffing of 5 cups of stale bread, 4 tablespoonsful of chopped onion, 1/2 teaspoonful of powdered basil, some chopped parsley, two beaten eggs and three cups of chewed (cream-style) corn. Spread stuffing on steaks. With packet thread and a larding needle draw flesh together of each steak. Then wrap each in a corn husk and tie these also. Bake 1/2 hour in a hot oven (400°) then reduce heat to 350° and bake another 20 minutes to the pound.

CHARLESTOWN

MACCARONI PIE

Boil 1 pound of maccaroni about 20 minutes until tender. Drain thoroughly until cool. Put into bowl and add 1 tablespoonful of butter, 1 teaspoonful of salt, 1 teaspoonful of mustard (prepared) and 1/8 teaspoon of nutmeg. Add 1 egg, well beaten. Then add 1/2 cup of milk and 2 cups of grated Parmesan cheese. Stir in 1/8 teaspoonful of black pepper with a few grains of red pepper mixed in with it. Turn the whole into a well buttered baking dish and bake. (At 350° until top is brown).

CREAM CHEESE COOKIES

Blend 3 ounces of cream cheese with 1/4 pound of butter and 1/4 cup of sugar. Blend in 1 teaspoonful of vanilla flavoring. Then add 1/2 cup of flour. Form into a long, log-like roll, wrap in a clean muslin cloth and place in a metal container in an ice container. Let remain overnight. Slice the dough very thin. Upon each cookie place some almonds and candied cherries. A hot oven (375°) is necessary for 10 minutes. The cookies will sizzle when done.

CHARLESTOWN

MAPLE PECAN CAKE

Sift 2 cups of flour with 4 teaspoonsful of baking powder. Cream 2 tablespoonsful of butter, add 1 cup of sugar and 1 cup of milk. Add 1 unbeaten egg and beat. Then add the flour and beat thoroughly. (300 strokes). Add vanilla. Bake in layer pans (at 375° for 25 minutes.)

ICING FOR PECAN CAKE

Beat the white of an egg until it stands alone in peaks, then slowly add, while beating, finely crushed (powdered) sugar. Flavor with 1 teaspoonful of maple flavoring. Decorate the cake with pecans.

SWEET PICKLED GOOSEBERRIES

Use 6 pounds of gooseberries to 1 pint of vinegar. Remove hanging blossom ends from gooseberries, then add the vinegar and 6 pounds of sugar. Carefully cook for 40 minutes. When done seal in crocks.

CHEESE WITH COWSLIP PETALS

Use unskimmed milk and let sour. When thick put into cheese cloth bag and let liquid drain off by hanging it over a basin in a cool room. Then salt the cheese when it is a solid mass, add some cowslip petals and put into a heart-shaped mold. After removing from mold pour thick cream over cheese before serving.

Smith's Townhouse in Boston
Where the Abolitionists Met

22

BOSTON

At their Boston home the Smiths joined in the anti-slavery movement then sweeping the country. Their home became a gathering place for prominent Abolitionists who were invited to dinner. Mary Ellen soon had a knowledge of New England cookery to which she added addtional seasonings quite her own.

To creamed clabber (cottage cheese) she added flower petals of marigolds, first pouring hot water over them and then crushing them to extract their slightly bitter taste. Then, after putting the unsalted clabber in a bowl, she sprinkled the mixture with brown sugar and with nutmeg. To sauces for fish she added the petals of lemon verbena, giving the dish a subtle but lemon-like flavor.

BOSTON

NEW ENGLAND ABOLITIONIST BEANS

Cover 2 pounds of beans (navy) with water and let remain overnight. In the morning heat the beans but do not boil. When water begins to get warm stir in 1 teaspoonful of baking soda. Remove from heat and run cold water over beans. Cover with water and boil ten minutes. Place in a bean pot. Put a large peeled onion in the center, 1 pound of salt pork, cut into squares of 1" x 2". Add 2/3 cup of dark molasses, 2 teaspoonsful of dry mustard, 2 teaspoonsful of salt, 8 tablespoonsful of brown sugar and 1/4 teaspoonful of dried ginger. Cover mixture with boiling water. Bake at 300° for six hours, adding hot water whenever liquid falls below the level of the beans.

BOSTON CLAM PIE

Melt 1 tablespoonful of butter, add 1 minced onion and lightly brown. Remove from pan and put in baking dish with 2 cups of minced clams and 1/4 cup of clam liquor. Add 1 well beaten egg and 1 cup of milk and some salt and pepper and then 1/2 cup of bread crumbs. Cover the mixture with pie crust and bake at 350° until the crust is nicely brown. If more flavoring is desired a 1/4 of a teaspoonful of thyme may be added and 1/4 cup of sherry.

BROWNSTONE FRONT CAKE

Pour 1 cup of boiling water over 3 squares (present commercial type) of chocolate, add 1 teaspoonful of soda and set in a warm place to dissolve. Cream 1/2 cup of butter with 2 cups of brown sugar. Add 2 egg yolks, slightly beaten, and 1/2 cup of sour milk. Sift together 2 1/2 cups of fine flour with 1 teaspoonful of baking powder and 1/4 teaspoonful of salt. Stir well into mixture. Add the dissolved chocolate and 1/4 teaspoonful of vanilla. Beat the whites of the two eggs until stiff and fold into mixture. Put the cake into a square pan, 9" x 9", and bake (at 350°) until a stiff straw thrust into cake comes out clean.

BOSTON

GOOSEBERRY CUSTARD TARTS

Remove blossom and stems from 1 pint of goose-berries. Cook until soft in water enough just to cover them. Then press the berries through a sieve. Add to them 3/4 cup of sugar and simmer for 3 or 4 minutes. Meanwhile make a custard by combining 2 egg yolks, 1 cupful of milk and 1/4 cupful of sugar. Put the custard mixture over boiling water (in a double boiler) and cook until it thickens. Remove from heat until cool, then mix with the gooseberry pulp. Arrange flaky pie crust in patty shells and fill with the gooseberry custard. Bake (350°) until the crust is lightly brown. Make a meringue of the 2 egg whites beaten with 4 table-spoonsful of granulated sugar and 1/4 teaspoonful of vanilla. Top custard with meringue and return to oven to lightly brown meringue.

FOR PATTY SHELLS

Beat 1 egg and add 1/2 cup of sugar, blending until smooth. Add 1 1/2 cups of fine flour which has been sifted. First chill the dough then roll it out very thin. Cut into circles and press against the backs of tart forms. Bake for 10 minutes (at 375°).

After James Smith's death in 1844 Mary Ellen married John James Plaissance, an almost white Negro from Richmond, Virginia. With him she engaged in Abolition activities for eight years, acting as an agent of the Underground Railway, the stations of which became the escape points from slave territory.

The time came when, having fortunately escaped a trap that had been laid for her capture, she had to flee. She took refuge with Marie Laveau, the Voodoo Queen of New Orleans. Mary Ellen's position as an agent remained perilous and under Marie's guidance the Underground agent was turned into an accomplished cook. Mary Ellen never ceased to wonder at the way Marie's friends disregarded with indifference the sumptuous dishes prepared in plantation kitchens. Only a few of the dishes served in the Voodoo Queen's household appealed to Mary Ellen. She actually disliked the "punkin-butter" which was pumpkin stewed with melon juice, "boiled down close." Nor did she like the claret mixed with cinnamon and herbs so often served there.

Home of Marie Laveau
Voodoo Queen of New Orleans
Where Mammy Took Refuge

NEW ORLEANS VOODOO

WUSSER MEAT CHAIN SAUSAGES

Mince very fine a leg of pork, allowing almost as much fat as meat. Weigh the resultant amount. Then for every 4 pounds add 2 1/2 ounces of salt, 1/2 ounce of pepper, twelve whole cloves, a dozen blades of mace, powdered, 2 grated nutmegs, 2 tablespoonsful of powdered sage and 2 teaspoonsful of powdered rosemary. Put it down into a jar and press the sausage hard. Clean casing with salt and vinegar after washing it. Then fill the casing tightly, securing into a chain of sausages of equal length tied with packet thread. Then put the sausages down into a brine (heavily salted water) so strong it will float an egg. Turn them daily for three weeks. Remove them, wipe dry and smoke them. When sufficiently smoked rub with sweet oil. For a time they may be preserved in the ashes of vine twigs. A few diced cranberries can be added to the sausage meat or dried wild cherries if a somewhat bitter taste is desired.

HOMINY GRITS AND CHEESE

Cook 1 quart of chopped-up collards. Add 1 cup of cooked hominy grits to drained collards. Then add 1 cup of yellow cheese and 2 tablespoonsful of butter and 2 tablespoonsful of tomata catchup (tomato catsup). Bake in the oven (at 350°) until a crust forms on top.

NEW ORLEANS VOODOO

CHITTERLINGS ON ST. ANN STREET

Select only the whitest pork chitterlings. Wash and cut into small pieces and place in a stew pan with 2 quarts of water. Bring to a boil and boil for 2 hours or more. After the first hour add 10 white onions cut fine. Add 2 tablespoonsful of butter, 2 tablespoonsful of cream and a sprinkling of nutmeg. Set the pan onto hot coals and boil until the chitterlings are quite tender. Add salt to taste and season with vinegar.

VOODOO MAGIC

Chop together very fine 3 pounds of lean veal with 1/2 pound of salt pork. Grate into it 1 nutmeg, 1 small onion, a very little salt and a flick of red pepper. Then add 3 well beaten eggs with 1 cup of milk. Shape into a loaf and press bread crumbs over it. Bake for 2 1/2 hours (at 350°.) Boil a cabbage and drain it, at the same time in another container boiling 6 potatoes. Mince the cabbage and the potatoes. Mix together with butter the size of an egg, some salt and pepper. Place around the meat when ready to serve.

LOUISIANA PLANTATION

River Road Plantation House near New Orleans

32

LOUISIANA PLANTATION

Mary Ellen found employment on a plantation on the River Road near New Orleans as a freed negro. With that adaptability which marked her character she settled down into a life where she was not the mistress measuring out the day's supply from the smokehouse, the shelf-lined storeroom and the wine safe on the back piazza, but the servant.

LOUISIANA PLANTATION

BLACK BEAN SOUP

Soak 3 cups of black beans overnight in cold water. Drain. Cover with cold water, add a ham bone, 2 peppercorns and 3 whole cloves and 1/4 tablespoon of allspice. Cook all day. When soup is done grate a hard-boiled egg into it, salt and pepper to taste and serve with wafer-thin slices of lemon floating on top.

LOUISIANA LAMB

Remove bone from a leg of mutton (lamb), take off outer skin and tie with packet thread. Squeeze a lemon over the whole, season with 1 teaspoonful of salt, 1 teaspoonful of parsley and flick very lightly with red pepper. Pour a glassful of currant jelly over the whole. Cook until done with 1/4 cupful of hot water in bottom of the pan. (Heat for 1/2 hour at 400° then thereafter cook 20 minutes to the pound at 350°). The meat should be a golden brown.

RIVER ROAD VEAL

Remove excess fat from 2 pounds of veal and cut up. Sear the meat in 2 tablespoonsful of fat, adding a little meat at a time. Add 1 large onion, cut fine, and cook until light brown. Add 1/2 teaspoonful of salt, one bay leaf (small) and 1/4 teaspoonful of thyme. Allow to steam for a few minutes over low heat covered. Then add 1 1/2 cups of hot water and 1/2 cup of beef broth and simmer for 1 hour. Add 3/4 cup of bread crumbs and simmer for another hour being careful that it does not burn. Just before serving add 1/2 cup of sweet cream and 1/4 pound of already cooked mushrooms. (A 1/2 teaspoonful of paprika improves the dish).

LOUISIANA PLANTATION

SPOON BREAD

Scald 1 cup of white cornmeal with 1 cup of boiling water. Stir in 1 tablespoonful of butter, 1/2 teaspoonful of salt and add 1 well beaten egg. Add 1 cup of rich milk and 1 1/2 teaspoonsful of baking powder. Mix well and put into a well-buttered bake pan. Bake for 40 minutes (350°). Serve with melted butter and maple syrup.

CORN BATTER CAKES

Mix 2 cups of sifted cornmeal with 1/2 cup of wheat flour and 2 teaspoonsful of baking powder with 1/2 teaspoon of salt. Add 1 egg to 1 1/4 cups of milk (more or less) and stir into the dry ingredients. Finally add 1 tablespoonful of melted butter. The dough should be soft. Bake as any other griddle cake and serve with maple syrup.

A typical Plantation Kitchen

LOUISIANA PLANTATION

BEATEN BISCUIT

Sift 1 quart of flour onto a tray, adding 1/2 tea-spoonful of salt. Cut into the flour a cupful of very cold lard. Wet with ice water to make a stiff dough. Lay the dough out on a floured board and give it 100 strokes with a rolling pin. Fold over and beat again until the dough becomes smooth and pliable. Then roll it out 1/2 inch thick and cut with a round cutter. Prick dough rounds with a fork. Bake to a delicate brown (at 350°).

DEVILED CRAB

Chop 2 small onions and saute in 2 tablespoonsful of butter. Add 1 tablespoonful of Worcestershire sauce, a dash of cayenne and 1 tablespoonful of chopped parsley. Add 1/2 cup of heavy cream and 1 level tablespoonful of prepared mustard. When smoothly cooked add 1 pint of flaked crab-meat. Stir in 1 chopped hard-boiled egg. Fill baking shells, cover with buttered crumbs (1 cupful is sufficient). Be sure to cover the edges of the shells. Bake 1/2 hour (at 350°) until well browned.

LOUISIANA PLANTATION

NEW ORLEANS SHRIMP

Cook 1/2 of a sliced onion in 2 tablespoonsful of butter until golden. Add 7 ounces of cleaned, already cooked shrimp. Add 1 cup of cream, 1 tablespoonful of Worcestershire sauce, 2 table-spoonsful of catchup, 1/4 teaspoonful of salt and 1/8 teaspoonful of pepper. Pour mixture into individual shells and top with buttered crumbs. Bake from 20 to 30 minutes (at 300°).

QUINCE PUDDING

Pare and scrape 6 quinces into a pulp. Mix the pulp with 1/2 pint of cream and 1/2 pound of sugar (powdered), stirring together very hard. Beat the yolks of 7 eggs together with 2 egg whites. Gradually stir the beaten eggs into the quince mixture and add 2 ordinary-sized wine glasses of rose water. Stir the whole very thoroughly and bake in a buttered dish. Bake for 3/4 of an hour (at 350°).

LOUISIANA PLANTATION

PERSIMMON PUDDING

Sift and resift 1 1/4 cups of flour. Add 1/4 tea-spoonful of salt, 1/2 teaspoonful of cinnamon, 1 cup of raisins and 1/2 cup of nuts. In a separate bowl combine 1 cup of persimmon pulp, 3/4 cup of sugar, 1 1/2 teaspoonsful of vanilla and 2 table-spoonsful of melted butter. Combine the ingredients. Pour into a greased bake dish and place down in a pan of hot water to cook in the oven (at 350°) for 1 1/4 hours.

ROSE GERANIUM CAKE

Measure out 1 cup of sweet (unsalted) butter and wrap about it cleanly washed rose geranium leaves. Leave out overnight in kitchen. In the morning remove the leaves and blend the butter with 2 cup-fuls of (finely granulated) sugar. Alternately stir in one cupful of milk and three cupfuls of flour to which has been added 3 teaspoonsful of baking powder. Beat well. Fold in 6 egg whites stiffly beaten. Bake in the oven until straw inserted into cake comes out clean. (This cake is best baked in layers at 350° from 20 to 30 minutes.)

FROSTING FOR ROSE GERANIUM CAKE

Dissolve 1 cup of sugar in 1/2 cup of hot water and boil rapidly to the thread stage. Let stand 2 or 3 minutes, then pour in a steady stream over the stiffly beaten whites of 2 eggs, constantly beating. Continue to beat until the frosting is cold and thick. Flavor with 1/4 teaspoonful of almond extract.

Mary Ellen's outstanding qualities as a cook soon became her undoing. If she remained on the River Road plantation she would eventually be identified as an agent of the Underground. Plaissance, who had changed his name to Pleasants, had already gone to California and Mary Ellen, dressed as a Quakeress, escaped to San Francisco. Her arrival was anticipated because she was referred to as "the greatest cook to ever come out of New Orleans." Men who had become wealthy in the California Gold Rush contested for her services. She accepted employment with the bachelors of the Case-Heiser commission house who had a large house on Washington Street.

To Mrs. Pleasants' surprise she had made available to her nearly everything she needed to enhance her reputation. She made daily raids upon the commission house. There were English dairy cheese in tins, oranges from Tahiti, cinnamon bark from Ceylon, tumeric from China, codfish from New England in wooden pails, oysters from Puget Sound, West Indies molasses and East Indian citron. Her bachelors procured for her meats from the single downtown butcher. The milk available was dirty and watered. Eggs were three dollars a dozen if they could be obtained. Always one to face up to any difficulty, Mary Ellen soon settled these problems herself by buying a place in the country. Her tenant farmers were soon supplying her with such "garden truck" as white stone turnips, drum-head cabbages and even radishes and rhubarb.

Fleeing to San Francisco,
Mammy Became the Housekeeper
for the Bachelors Operating
the Commission House of Case Heiser

SAN FRANCISCO BACHELOR CLUB

CROWN ROAST OF LAMB

Strip a rack of lamb ribs of meat down to the meaty part of the chops. Then with the bone sides turned outward form into a crown and secure by sewing flesh together with a larding needle. Into the hollow center put the following filling. Grind 3 pounds of lamb shank meat stripped from the bones. Brown 2 small onions in 3 tablespoonsful of oil together with 1 cup of white bread crumbs. Add 1/2 cup of already cooked rice, 1 cup of cream, 2 eggs, unbeaten, 1/2 teaspoonful of nutmeg, 1 tablespoonful of salt and 1/2 teaspoonful of pepper. Braid the outside of the crown basket-fashion with strips of fat. Heat the roast through in a hot oven for 15 minutes (450° then reduce heat to 350° and cook 20 minutes to the pound).

SAN FRANCISCO BACHELOR CLUB

BACHELOR CLUB CHICKEN

Place 6 breasts of chicken in a deep dish. Mix 1 cup of oil (olive), 1/2 teaspoonful of leaf oregano, 1/2 teaspoonful of basil, 1/2 teaspoonful of rosemary leaves, 1/2 teaspoonful of cumin. (To improve dish add 1/2 teaspoonful of paprika, 1/2 teaspoonful of garlic powder and 1/2 teaspoonful of Italian seasoning.) Add salt and pepper. Pour the herb seasoned oil over the chicken breasts and marinate for 6 hours. Meanwhile prepare a dressing. Fry 2 slices of thick bacon and mince. Add 4 tablespoonsful of chopped celery leaves. Add 4 cups of broken up cornmeal bread and 1 cup of chicken broth. Add 2 beaten eggs. Put aside with one large onion sliced into rings. Place the rings over the dressing and some over the chicken breasts. Put the stuffing under the breasts in a well greased pan, place onion rings on breasts and bake for 45 minutes (at 350° for 20 minutes and 300° thereafter.)

TURTLE STEW

Everything was done to please the autocrat of the Case-Heiser kitchen. Mary Ellen demanded and got one of the new squat kitchen ranges. The proprietor of a restaurant had been importing turtles from the Galapagos Islands for a year. One day when one hundred of them that he had obtained escaped and were seen swimming away to the Farrallones the restaurant keeper resorted to thereafter preserving the turtle meat. The bachelors paid an exorbitant price to supply Mrs. Pleasants with this item.

Thicken the stock from 4 cups of turtle meat with flour. Add a wine glass of sherry and 1/8 cup of lemon juice. Into the sauce put 1 teaspoonful of allspice and 1/2 teaspoonful of mace. Add turtle meat. Put 2 whole cloves in and heat and serve in a chafing dish.

SAN FRANCISCO BACHELOR CLUB

PORCUPINE QUILLS

Spread a sponge cake over with raspberry jam and place blanched almonds upright in it. Pour rum over the cake and serve with a liquid custard.

LIQUID CUSTARD

Scald 2 cups of milk (in a double boiler). Beat 2 eggs slightly, adding 1/8 teaspoonful of salt, 4 tablespoonsful of sugar and 1/2 teaspoonful of vanilla. Remove the hot milk from over the heat and add to the egg mixture. After thoroughly mixing return to heat (in double boiler). Cook until egg coats a spoon, meanwhile constantly stirring mixture.

RASPBERRY VINEGAR

Put 2 quarts of fresh raspberries into a stone crock. Pour over the berries a quart of vinegar. After a period of twenty-four hours strain the mixture through a sieve. Then pour the liquid over 2 more quarts of raspberries and let stand for another 24 hours. Strain once more. Allow 1 pound of sugar to every pint of juice and let it stand until it melts in the liquor. Then put the liquid in a closely covered kettle set down into boiling water and keep the water boiling for an hour. Remove any scum that might have gathered on the surface. Bottle for use when cold. Mix with water to serve as a drink, heated if the weather is cold.

SUNDAY
DINNER
IN THE
COUNTRY

SUNDAY DINNER

After nineteen months the Case-Heiser partners went into other ventures and the club disbanded. For a time Mary Ellen acted as a maid to the bride of one of the bachelors. While between jobs she decided to take a vacation at her farm, Geneva Cottage. Mrs. Pleasants had used money inherited from Smith to open three laundries, one of the most profitable of all businesses of the period. She had decided that Thomas F. Bell, whom she had met on the way to California, was an astute financier. She invited him to her country place for Sunday dinner to discuss with him the placing of her considerable capital in his hands for investment.

Mammy Acquired a Country Place
Which She Called Geneva Cottage

SUNDAY DINNER

GENEVA COTTAGE BEEF

Use the first four ribs of a quartering of beef. Braise the standing rib roast of beef in a frying pan to seal in the juice. Place on a rack in a roasting pan with the fat side up. Heat through (at 400°) for half an hour. Reduce heat and cook 18 minutes to the pound for rare beef (at 350°). While the roast is cooking baste with the following: Mix 2 tablespoonsful of Worcestershire sauce with 4 tablespoonsful of melted butter and 1 teaspoonful of finely grated horseradish.

HORSERADISH SAUCE FOR BEEF

Mix 2 tablespoonsful of finely grated horseradish with 2 tablespoonsful of sour cream. Add 1 teaspoonful of white wine, 1/8 teaspoonful of black pepper and 1 teaspoonful of mustard.

NASTURTIUM ARTIFICE

Select nasturtiums in assorted colors. Carefully wash them, remove pistels in centers and stems. Arrange on a plate and fill cavities with following mixture. Mix 1/2 cup of cooked Oregon salmon with 1/4 cup of cream cheese and add 1/8 teaspoonful of marjoram.

CARAWAY SEED CHEESE

Measure out 8 ounces of cream cheese and work into it 1/4 cup of soft butter. When smooth add 1 teaspoonful of capers, 1/2 teaspoonful of caraway seed and 1/2 teaspoonful of salt. Finally add 4 Norway sardines that have been packed in olive oil. (A teaspoonful of paprika improves the cheese). Finally put into a mold and leave in a cold place overnight. Then remove from mold.

SUNDAY DINNER

GLAZED CARROTS

Cook carrots until almost tender. Roll in sugar. Then simmer in melted butter, turning often, until glazed. Just before removing from pan sprinkle with lemon juice and powdered thyme.

RHUBARB COBBLER

Line a deep dish with short pie crust (see patty shells page 25) rolled at least 1/4 inch thick. Prick all over with a fork. Prepare 1 quart of rhubarb with 1 1/2 cups of water and 2 1/2 cups of sugar, boiling for 15 minutes. Remove from the fire and add the well beaten yolks of 4 eggs. Mix well together and pour into the shell and bake in a moderate oven (350°). When shell is nicely baked beat the whites of the eggs to a stiff froth, together with 2 tablespoonsful of sugar, apply to the top of the cobbler and brown lightly.

PINK PEARS

Hollow out cooked pear halves. Marinate them in the liquid from sweet pickled beets. Fill the hollows with white grapes which have the seeds removed. Pit dark red cherries with a quill feather and put among grapes. Then shred a small amount of candied ginger and spread across the tops. Finally place the pears down into a sea of whipped cream.

CANDIED VIOLET PETALS

Gently wash the petals of a bunch of violets, then let the petals dry. Boil 1/2 pound of sugar with 1/2 pint of water. Boil until it spins a thread. Then, holding each violet by the stem, dip it down into the hot syrup, lay on a slightly oiled screen and let stand. If the violets emerge looking clear a second dipping will not be necessary.

GOLD RUSH COOKING

*Mammy designed this house for one of her proteges,
Laura Wilson. It was moved to 116 Laidley Street
from its original site on Maiden Lane.*

GOLD RUSH COOKING

Mary Ellen next became the cook for another bachelor club headed by Selim and Fred Woodworth, wealthy financiers and social leaders. It was her plan to open a series of fashionable boarding houses and through her association with this club she was given the opportunity to meet the men she wished to have as patrons. Her prestige as a cook also expanded because the brothers owned Red Rock Island and provided her with game.

Many men who brought shipments into the thriving city never had an opportunity to visit the gold country. It amused Fred to have served at the table the dishes characteristic of the Mother Lode. Even more eccentric were the dishes suggested by Selim. He was acting as consul for China and introduced Mary Ellen to dishes more exotic than actually Oriental.

GOLD RUSH COOKING

MARY ELLEN'S FAVORITE DISH

(Originally a Chinese dish, Mrs. Pleasants adapted it to her own liking and it became the dish most often requested. Because it can be kept warm indefinitely it is a perfect choice for buffet suppers.) Eventually the dish had a name, acquired in the late 1860s. It was called *Bonanza Stew*.

Two of the component parts of the dish, the liquor and the noodles must be prepared a day in advance.

THICK NOODLES

Beat 2 eggs with a fork. Add a teaspoonful of water and 1/4 teaspoonful of salt. Stir in flour until moisture is all but absorbed. Roll out but not too thinly. Cut into strips and allow to entirely dry out overnight. When ready to use boil rapidly in salted water. The noodles are done when they are cooked through to softness.

MAMMY'S BONANZA STEW

Render out pork fat to the amount of 4 table-spoonsful (not salt pork). Put the grease into a very large frying pan and add 4 small sliced onions. When these have begun to brown add 2 cups of finely cut celery and 2 cut-up green peppers. When the celery begins to look a little transparent start to add six cupsful of the finest pork tenderloin cut into small strips, letting the pieces brown. Then remove the meat mixture into a large stew kettle. Add 1 cup of uncooked white rice and 1 1/2 teaspoonsful of salt. Add enough of the already prepared liquor to just cover the meat and rice mixture. Then stir into it 2 tablespoonsful of Worcestershire sauce. Bring liquid to the boiling point, cover, reduce heat and continue cooking. As the rice swells more and more liquor has to be added. The dish is done when the pork tenderloin is easily broken. Toward the end the dish should be nicely moist but not swimming in the liquor. Just before removing from the heat add 1 cupful of sliced, and 1 cupful of whole cooked mushrooms. Serve on platter surrounded by cooked noodles.

Liquor for Dish

Put 10 cups of water into a stew kettle. Add 2 cups of well seasoned beef stock. Put into the liquid 1/2 pound of stewing beef cut into very small pieces. Add 1 cup each of carrots, potatoes, tomatoes, peas, green beans. Add 1/2 cup of diced onions and 1/2 cup of barley, 10 blades of fresh chives, and 1/4 heaping teaspoonful of dried chervil. Cook until the meat is tender. Then mash the mixture and push through the sieve of a colander. Set aside in a large bowl.

GOLD RUSH COOKING

DUCK WITH BARLEY DRESSING

When duck is prepared for oven remove the entire neck to enlarge space for dressing. Use 3 cups of cooked barley. Fry 2 pieces of bacon and mince. Add 1/2 cup of celery tops and 3 tablespoonsful of onion. Mix into barley. In a small bowl blend 1/4 teaspoonful of thyme, 1/8 teaspoonful of sage, 1/4 teaspoonful of marjoram, 1/4 teaspoonful of rosemary, 1/2 teaspoonful of salt, 1/8 teaspoonful of pepper and 1/8 teaspoonful of nutmeg. Scatter over barley and mix in. Add 1 well whipped egg and 1/2 cup of chicken broth. Finally add 3 tablespoonsful of melted butter. Stuff the duck and sew up openings. Place on a rack in a roasting pan. Heat in a hot oven (450° for 15 minutes) then reduce to moderate heat (350°. The bird should be cooked at 25 minutes to the pound). To the gravy made from the juice add a few oysters and some chopped pecans. (Avoid commercial poultry seasoning).

BACHELOR CLUB PHEASANT

Since a pheasant is apt to be dry if improperly cooked it is well to butter the entire inside. Upon the outside secure slices of bacon which should be taken off when the bird is nearly finished. Bake in a moderate oven. (at 350°. The usual pheasant does not take more than 1 1/2 hours to cook.) To the gravy add a wine glass of claret and the juice of 2 oranges, the latter being added just before serving.

GOLD RUSH COOKING

OPHIR MINE BEANS

Add 5 cups of water to 2 cups of spotted beans (fresh hulled cranberry beans are best). Stir in 1/2 pound of chopped (ground) beef and several small hunks of bacon. Add 2 onions and 3 tomatoes, cut into slices, and some salt and pepper. (The addition of a cut-up green pepper improves the dish). Boil until until beans are soft.

HANGTOWN FRY

Thoroughly drain 1 pint of oysters. Simmer them in 2 tablespoonsful of butter until their edges begin to curl. Break into the frying pan 6 eggs and stir in 1/3 cup of cream. Cook slowly and stir to keep the mixture from sticking to the pan. Add salt and pepper just before removing from fire.

POTTED HARE, RED ROCK ISLAND STYLE

Have one hare cut into joints. Roll in oatmeal which has been well crushed with a rolling pin. Dust the joints over with salt and pepper. Lightly fry the pieces in shortening and put them down into a deep dish. Next melt 3 tablespoonsful of butter over low heat and add 1 small onion well chopped. Into a cheesecloth bag tied with a string put 2 leaves of thyme, 2 bay leaves, 2 marjoram leaves and some chopped up parsley. Place this in dish with hare and pour 1 glassful of burgundy wine over it together with 4 cups of beef broth. While cooking the dish must be covered tightly and placed down into a larger pan of boiling water. Cook until meat begins to fall off the bone.

CHINESE PUDDING

Soak 2 1/2 slices of white bread in water. Then squeeze the bread dry and crumble it into bits. Next caramelize 2 tablespoonsful of sugar and add to it 1 pint of hot milk and stir until sugar is dissolved. Then stir in the bread crumbs and add 4 table-spoonsful of granulated sugar. Next add 2 well beaten eggs. Stir in 2 tablespoonsful of melted butter, 1/2 teaspoonful of salt and 1/4 cup of preserved ginger. Finally add 2 tablespoonsful of ginger syrup. Beat mixture together and bake slowly (300°) until nicely brown.

The Schell House at Schellville,
built by Mammy for the sister of
Fred and Selim Woodworth

59

RIVER BOAT FARE

RIVER BOAT FARE

Selim and Fred Woodworth finally disbanded the club and moved to adjoining iron houses on Minna Street. Fred went East to bring his mother and sisters out to San Francisco and Selim was married at this same time. Mary Ellen was to continue on as Selim's housekeeper but during the absence of the brothers the River Kings asked if they might "borrow" her for the summer months. Mrs. Pleasants' temporary employers owned two navigation companies operating steamers on the inland waterways. They were concerned with her improving the bill of fare aboard such river boats as the *Senator* and the *New World* rather than having any interest in the make-shift club they maintained across from the wharf they owned. Mary Ellen was soon travelling aboard the elegantly fitted up *Senator* with its perforated fretwork and elegant fittings. She taught the negro cooks to become first rate chefs, including her own husband. But she took time out to enjoy the splendid hill scenery, the woodlands and the many ranchos on the route to Sacramento City. And she might have dreamed of the day when she would be worth fifteen million dollars.

Typical River Boat

RIVER BOAT FARE

TRIMMED STEAK

Select 2 flank steaks of 2 pounds each. Score both sides of the steaks with lightly cut criss-cross cuttings to soften tough grain of meat. Rub into steaks 1 cup of flour that has 2 teaspoonsful of salt mixed in with it. Put the steaks down into an iron pot.

Pour over the meat a mixture composed of 1 cup of water, 1 cup of mild vinegar, 12 whole allspice, 6 whole cloves, 1 teaspoonful of celery seed and 1 teaspoonful of thyme, preheated. Tightly cover pot with iron lid and cook very slowly over low heat until tender.

RIVER BOAT FARE

YERBA BUENA POT

Select a large chicken (4 pounds at least) and cut up. With it put a veal knuckle bone. Place both in a pot containing 3 quarts of boiling water. Let come to a boil again and then simmer until the breast of the chicken is tender. Then add the following: 1 quart of corn freshly cut from the cobs, 4 whole onions, 1 quart of dried tomatoes (fresh tomatoes, halved), 2 sweet green peppers, (cut up), 1 pound of green beans tied in small bunches with palm fiber (rafia) and 6 summer squashes. Put in a washed whole apple and a hard pear for flavoring. Add salt and pepper to taste. Cook just until chicken is finished, adding at the last 10 blades of cut-up chives, 4 ounces of tomato paste and 1/4 teaspoonful of chervil. (Celery seed, onion powder, and monosodiumglutamate may be added if a stronger flavor is desired.) Strain off the broth, remove knuckle bone and place the chicken and vegatables on a platter.

SWEET POTATO PONE

Without removing the peelings, wash thoroughly and scrape 8 sweet potatoes, then grate. Beat 2 eggs together and stir in 1/2 cup of brown sugar. Mix 1/2 cup of syrup with the potatoes, then stir in the sugar and eggs. Finally add 2 tablespoonsful of finely diced orange peel and 1 teaspoonful of cinnamon. Put in greased iron pone pan and bake to a delicate brown. (350°)

RIVER BOAT FARE

RIVER BOAT CAKE

Whip one cup of whipping cream until it is firm, then add 2 eggs, one at a time and beat to a light foam. Add 1 cup of sugar and beat again (this time changing from a rotary beater to a wire whip beater). Have ready, sifted together, 1 1/2 cups of flour, mixed with 2 teaspoonsful of baking powder and 1/4 teaspoonful of salt. Mix eggs and flour mixture until smooth and add 1 teaspoonful of vanilla. Bake in a tube pan (at 400°) for about 25 minutes. The hollow center of the cake may be filled with sugared fresh peaches or with fresh berries, topped with sweetened whipping cream.

DATE DESSERT, SENATOR STYLE

Separate the yolks of 4 eggs from the whites. Beat the egg yolks, gradually adding 1/2 cup of sugar. Then beat the egg whites adding another 1/2 cup of sugar. When the egg whites are stiff enough to stand in peaks fold them into the beaten yolks and add 1 teaspoonful of baking powder, 1 cupful of pitted dates, chopped into small pieces, and 1 cupful of chopped up walnuts. Bake slowly (300°) until properly brown. The dessert, cut into squares, is best served with sweetened, vanilla-flavored whipped cream.

RIVER KING SQUATUM

Returning to the Woodworths Mary Ellen oversaw the management of their adjoining houses. She inveigled them into giving a "squatum" or picnic, to which the River Kings were invited.

*After Leaving the Case-Heiser Bachelors' Club
Mammy managed the Twin Iron Houses of
Selim and Fred Woodworth on Minna Street in San Francisco*

RIVER KING SQUATUM

SMOKED PICNIC TONGUE

Cover a 5 pound smoked tongue with cold water. Put into the water 3 small onions, 1 bay leaf, 8 whole black peppers and 1/4 teaspoonful of salt. Bring to a boil then reduce heat to simmer for at least 4 hours. When the tongue is tender trim off the roots and gristle. Peel off the skin when it has cooled and cut tongue into thin slices.

SQUATUM QUAIL

Select the six best quail the hunter has brought in. After they are ready for the oven butter them inside and also salt and pepper. Truss the birds with slices of bacon and wrap them in grape leaves. Pour melted butter and the juice of a lemon over them and put a little boiling water in the bottom of the pan. Then roast for 30 minutes. (400°). Serve cold with spiced guava.

CHEESE SANDWICH

Over buttered thin slices of nut bread spread grated Edam cheese which has been softened with sherry. (Blend in some paprika and a little pepper.)

BAKED HAM

Bake a ham in sweet cider, basting the meat with the cider and keeping the ham covered to keep it moist. After baking it a sufficient time (400° for half an hour and 350° at 20 minutes to the pound) remove cover. Carefully cut off the skin and spread layer of fat with beaten egg yolk mixed with brown sugar. Push back into the oven long enough for the egg to become a golden brown. Let the ham get cold and thinly slice. Place the slices on a large oval dish. Decorate the outer edge of the plate by making roses of continuous, thin apple parings, pinked in beet juice, turned wrong side out and rolled up. For foliage use the real stems of roses. With the ham serve claret.

RIVER KING SQUATUM

BLACK CAKE

Put 1 pound of currants in boiling water and allow to boil for 2 minutes. Then spread them out to dry and finally dredge them with flour. Mix together 2 teaspoonsful of cinnamon, 1/2 tablespoonful of mace and 1/2 tablespoonful of nutmeg. Also mix together 1 glass of white wine, 1/2 glass of brandy and 1/2 glass of rose water. Cut 1/2 pound of citron into small pieces. Into a bowl measure out 1/2 pound of flour and into another bowl 1/2 pound of sugar (powdered). Into the bowl with the sugar cut 1/2 pound of butter and mash and stir until creamy. Beat 6 eggs until smooth, then stir into them gradually the butter and sugar mixture alternately with the flour. Then add the currants, citron, spices, and wine-brandy-rose water mixture. Stir very hard.

Either a little more moisture or a little more flour may be needed. The dough should be stiff but not runny. Grease loaf pans and line with heavy brown paper. Fill the pans 2/3 full and bake (at 275°). When straw comes out clean from cakes they are done. Upon removing them from oven tear off the paper, place on rack to cool and lightly dredge with flour. Wipe the flour off before icing the cake.

ICING FOR BLACK CAKE

Beat 2 egg whites until stiff. Add 1/2 pound of loaf sugar (powdered) and beat until it stands alone at the same time adding 1/2 teaspoonful of rose extract. (A little gum of tragacanth was always added to the icing to give it body).

COASTAL STEAMER COOKING

Mammy's Second Husband, Pleasants,
Became Cook on the Coastal Steamer Orizaba

COASTAL STEAMER COOKING

Mammy's husband, James, who had become a skilled cook when employed by the River Kings, finally became the chief cook aboard the coastal steamer, *Orizaba*, the only ship on the Coast with a walk-in ice house.

COASTAL STEAMER COOKING

APPLES-GONE-TO-HEAVEN

Core 6 apples, leaving their skins on. (Roman Beauties are best). Fill the reamed out centers with the following mixture: Mix 3 tablespoonsful of white raisins, 3 tablespoonsful of cut-up citron peel, 3 tablespoonsful of lemon peel to which has been added 3 tablespoonsful of brown sugar. When aperatures are filled pour over them 3 tablespoonsful of melted butter. Set the apples down into a baking dish with 1 cup of water in the bottom to which 1/4 cup of brown sugar has been added. While baking the apples (at 350°) keep basting them. They are done when a fork easily penetrates an apple's side.

EGGS ORIZABA

Grease cups of muffin tin. Break an egg into each one. Pour cream over the eggs until each hollow is filled. Bake until eggs harden and serve on rounds of bread (toasted).

74

COASTAL STEAMER COOKING

COASTAL STEAMER STEAK

To serve four people cut 2 pounds of round steak, 1 1/4" thick, and score the meat on both sides. Then spread the steak over with mustard (prepared) Put into a deep dish tomato sauce (chili sauce), 6 tablespoonsful of melted butter, 3 teaspoonsful of Worcestershire sauce, 1 teaspoonful of salt and 1/4 teaspoonful of pepper. Let the steak marinate in this mixture for 3 hours. Drain steak and brown in a hot skillet together with 1/2 pound of large, fresh mushrooms. When steak and mushrooms are nicely brown pour over them the sauce mixture into which has been put a cup of boiling water. Cover the skillet tightly and simmer for 1 hour.

LEMON PUDDING

Into 1/2 cup of flour put 1/2 teaspoonful of baking powder, together with 1/4 teaspoonful of salt. Beat the yolks of 3 eggs, then beat the whites separately. Add 1 1/2 cups of sugar to the egg yolks, stir in the whites, and then the flour mixture alternately with 1 1/2 cups of milk. Blend in 2 tablespoonsful of melted butter and finally add 2 teaspoonsful of grated lemon rind and 1/4 cup of lemon juice. Pour mixture into baking dish, set down into a shallow pan of hot water. Bake until firm and nicely browned (at 375° for 40 to 45 minutes). When turned out into a serving dish there will be a cake layer on top and a custard layer at the bottom. Serve with sweetened whipped cream.

MISSOURI

PLANTATION

In 1858 Mrs. Pleasants went East to meet the Abolitionist leader, John Brown, carrying with her a draft for $30,000 in the belief that Brown could successfully carry out the war against slavery. Mary Ellen met Brown at Chatham and gave him a purse with $500 in gold, collected from Negroes in California. Brown was later arrested for an unsuccessful raid on an army arsenal at which time Mary Ellen was going from plantation to plantation dressed as a jockey to arouse the slaves to revolt. She was forced to desist and took refuge with Judge Isaac Hunter, whose daughter had married Mary Ellen's liberator, Americus Price. Judge Hunter sent her to an adjoining plantation and it was there she began to be called Mammy Pleasant.

In 1859, with the Abolitionist John Brown,
Mammy Engaged in Running Slaves out
Over the Underground to Canada. She Was About
to be Captured and Fled
to the Hunter Plantation in Missouri

MISSOURI PLANTATION

SYLLABUB

Into a pint of sweet cider grate 1 whole nutmeg. Add 3 pints of milk and whip vigorously with blades (rotary beater). Serve before the froth subsides.

PERSIMMON BEER

Be sure the persimmons are fully ripe. Remove from them the stalk ends and the interior calyxes. Then mash the fruit and add enough wheat bran to make a stiff dough. Form the dough into thin flat cakes and bake until crisp. Then break the cakes up into clean wooden barrels and fill them with water. Set the barrels upright and cover them with thin white cloths and set them in a place which is warm and dry. The cakes will rise to the tops and begin to foam. Three or four weeks later the barrels must then be moved to a cold place and wooden covers put on them. (To make certain of success, toast dipped in yeast can be put into the barrels with the persimmon cakes.)

MISSOURI PLANTATION

PLANTATION BEAN POT

Use 2 quarts of fresh, black-eyed peas. Soak them overnight in salted water to overcome any dryness. In the morning place the peas in a large roaster, preferably of iron. Add 3/4 of a pound of salt pork, cut into several pieces. Cover the peas with a liquid mixture which is 1/2 water and 1/2 claret. Tie into a (cheesecloth) sack containing leaves of marjoram, thyme, laurel, and flowers of papayas, 3 cloves and 4 black peppers. Start in a hot oven until heated, then cook over slow heat. The liquid will boil away. As it does, add dry white wine. Before removing from the heat add 1 water glass of strong coffee. Remove from heat and add 2 tablespoonsful of brown sugar and 1/4 cup of brandy. The dish will take about 6 hours to cook.

HOPPIN' JOHN

Soak overnight 1 quart of fresh black beans. In the morning boil the beans until soft with 1 pound of bacon, cut into large cubes, and 1 bay leaf. When the beans are done add 3 cups of boiled rice to the dish and heat again. Strain off liquid and place on platter with bacon pieces on top.

MISSOURI PLANTATION

MOLASSES SPONGE CAKE

Beat the yolks of 4 eggs until light. Then gradually beat in 1/2 cup of molasses. Beat the egg whites to foamy consistency and add to this 1 teaspoonful of lemon juice. Gradually beat into the egg whites 6 tablespoonsful of sugar. Fold into the egg yolk mixture. Into 1 cup of flour put 1/2 teaspoonful of salt, 1 teaspoonful of cinnamon, 1/2 teaspoonful of nutmeg, 1/4 teaspoonful of mace. Put 1/2 teaspoonful of soda, moistened with water, into the egg mixture. Then begin to add the flour mixture slowly. (The cake is best baked in layers at 325° from 20 to 25 minutes). Fill with lemon filling.

LEMON FILLING

Mix together 4 egg yolks, 1/4 cup of lemon juice, 1 tablespoonful of lemon peel, grated, 1/3 cup of softened butter and 1/2 cup of sugar. Put the combination (in the top of a double boiler) over boiling water and cook until the mixture becomes thickened. When cool put between the layers of the cake. (A paper lace doily may be used to put a powdered sugar design on the top of the cake. The powdered sugar, sifted through the perforations, gives the cake an elegant look. Mary Ellen had to cut the doilies she used).

RINCON HILL MANSION

RINCON HILL MANSION

Returning to San Francisco Mary Ellen became the housekeeper for Fred Woodworth who had acquired a house on Folsom Street on Rincon Hill. Fred was currently the wealthiest man in San Francisco with an income of $1,000 a day from his Ophir mine. He was also one of the most popular men in the city. Together with a partner named Frederick Schell, he owned a piano business. As befitted the son of the man who had written *The Old Oaken Bucket*, Fred was an excellent musician and the wealthy and the famous gathered at his home not only to enjoy his lavish dinners but to hear him play the piano.

Fred Woodworth's House at 638 Folsom, San Francisco
Later the Home of Ex-Senator Milton Latham

RINCON HILL MANSION

SUCKLING PIG, ROASTED

First make the stuffing: to 8 cupsful of broken up stale bread, add 4 cups of chopped celery leaves, 2 large onions, chopped fine, 4 tablespoonsful of melted butter and 6 cups of cranberry sauce, some salt and pepper. A suckling pig three weeks old is used. After the pig has been drawn and scraped and thoroughly cleaned, the roast is ready for cooking. Cover the ears with muslin and secure to prevent them from being burned. Then grease a piece of muslin sufficient to entirely wrap up the roast. After heating it through for 1/2 hour (400°) allow 25 minutes to the pound for cooking (at 350°.) Keep adding hot water to the juice in the pan to prevent burning.

CHUTNEY TO ACCOMPANY ROAST PIG

Use 6 tomatoes. Hold them on fork briefly over a flame to loosen skins and then peel. Chop up the tomatoes. Add to them 6 apples (green Pippins) which have also been chopped up. Mix in 6 dried figs which have also been cut up into small pieces. Add to the mixture 1 whole clove and a small onion which has been grated. Then stir in 1/8 teaspoonful of ginger and just a flick of cayenne pepper and some salt. Then stir in 1/4 pound of brown sugar and 1 pint of vinegar. Boil the chutney for 1/2 hour. When completely cold seal into small stone jars.

RINCON HILL MANSION

SHAD ROE SAN FRANCISCO

Put the shad roe down into boiling water just sufficient to cover it. Simmer for 20 minutes, first
adding 1 tablespoonful of vinegar, a slice of onion
and 1/2 of a bay leaf. Drain and cover with cold
water for 5 minutes. Have, already prepared during
the time the fish roe was simmering, a sauce made
of 2 cups of strained stewed tomatoes, 4 tablespoonsful of melted butter and 1 sliced onion. Place
the roe down in a buttered pan and put the tomato
sauce around it. Baste the roe with the sauce while
cooking for 20 minutes in a moderate oven (350°).
Remove roe to a heated dish. Place the sauce into a
frying pan and over low heat stir into it 2 tablespoonsful of flour which has been smoothly mixed
into a little water. Add 1 tablespoonful of Worcestershire sauce and stir until the sauce thickens, then
pour the sauce over the roe.

RINCON HILL ROAST

First make a marinade to improve the flavor of the
beef. Use the juice of 2 lemons and in this place 2
tablespoonsful of parsley, 1 teaspoonful of peppercorns, 1 onion cut into rings, 1 bay leaf, a piece of
mace, and 1 stalk of celery. Next pound a 5 pound
roast of beef to break down any tough grains. Then
put the roast down into the pickling mixture and
keep turning the meat over every little while for 2
hours. Then take out the roast, rub some salt,
pepper and some flour on it together with 1/4
teaspoonful of nutmeg. Next roll the roast up and
tie with twine. Sear (at 500°) until brown on all
sides. Then reduce heat (to 350°) and pour marinade over the roast with 2 cloves of garlic placed
down into the liquor. Baste roast while cooking for
2 1/2 hours.

RINCON HILL MANSION

PATTY-CAKE VEAL

Grind up 2 pounds of veal, first cutting off any fat or strings of tough fiber. Mix into the veal 1/2 pound of salt pork which has also been ground. Add 2 beaten eggs, 1 cup of bread crumbs, and 1/2 pound of well-washed, chopped up mushrooms. Add to the mixture some pepper and 1/4 teaspoonful of nutmeg. Form meat into small patty-cakes. Sprinkle bread crumbs on both sides of the meat and place in a greased pan. Cook in slow oven (at 350°) until nicely brown.

SCALLOP-EDGED SUMMER SQUASH

Cut the cymlings, or squash, in halves and remove the seeded centers. Put down into boiling water and simmer for 10 minutes. Drain. Prepare the following stuffing: Prepare enough minced ham to fill the cymlings. Into this stir enough white sauce (see page 10) and raw egg yolk to moisten, adding small dices of green pepper, a small amount of salt and pepper (paprika if desired). Fill cavities of the vegetable, dot with bread crumbs and butter and bake until bread crumbs are brown.

RINCON HILL MANSION

ISLE-IN-THE-BAY

Beat the whites of 9 eggs until very stiff adding, a little at a time, 1/2 pound of powdered sugar, the grated rind of 1 lemon, and 3/4 pound of ground almonds. Then beat the yolks of the eggs until light and fluffy and add to the whites. Place the mixture in a mold and set down into boiling water in the oven for about 3/4 of an hour. Let cool, when done, and break up the molded egg mixture into pieces with a fork. Add to them a pint of sweetened whipped cream, 1/2 cup of diced, candied cherries and 1/2 cup of pecans. Thoroughly chill and then serve.

SUMMER-DAY SALAD

Cube sugared pineapple, bananas, and well-sugared grapefruit. (Canned fruits may be used, but only if well drained). Add grapes that have had the seeds removed. Make a dressing for the fruit as follows: Mix 1 well-beaten egg with 1/4 cup of sugar, 1/3 cupful of pineapple juice and 3 tablespoonsful of lemon juice. Cook over hot water (in double boiler) until smooth, stirring constantly. First chill and then fold into the dressing 1/2 cup of whipped cream. Toast and salt blanced pistachio nuts and use them as a garnish.

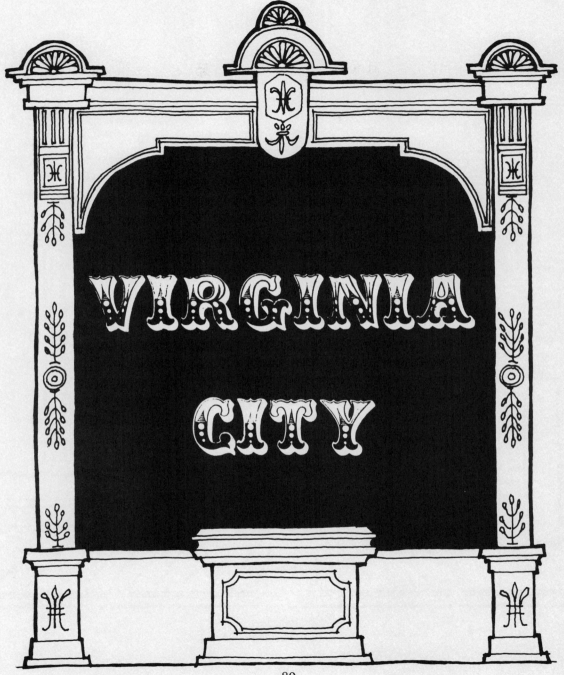

Chinese Peddler, Virginia City

VIRGINIA CITY

Virginia City was the most famous mining town in the world with a four-mile line of mines at the foot of Mount Davidson overlooking the town. Mammy had never seen the Ophir Mine but close to its shaft house and mills was a brick hotel maintained for the officers of the company. The place was noted for its "wine dinners" and although Mary Ellen was not there to oversee them the recipes used were hers.

One of the legends, characteristic of the Comstock Lode, concerned Mark Twain. Mark had, of course, tried his hand at mining but when he walked from Aurora to Virginia City to join the staff of *The Enterprise* at twenty-five dollars a week, he had come, as a famous writer once·said, "to claim his destiny."

But the capricious historian would tell the story otherwise. Mark Twain upon his arrival went to work in the Ophir at ten dollars a week. When he saw the extent of the output of the mine he asked for a raise. The superintendent of the company asked him how much more he wanted. Mark Twain replied that he'd be satisfied with ten thousand dollars a week provided he was served his meals at the Ophir "hotel."

VIRGINIA CITY

VENISON PASTRY

Cut venison steaks into small pieces. Put into boiling water to cover and stew for 25 minutes. Use rich pastry (see patty shells page 25) to line a baking dish. Place the drained venison in the dish. Thicken the liquor from the stew with 1 tablespoonful of arrowroot and add to venison. Add pepper and salt. Cover the dish with pastry and cut vents in the top. Bake (at 375°) until the pie crust is a golden brown.

ROAST GOOSE, CORN BREAD STUFFING

See that the plump young bird is well wiped after it has been washed. For the stuffing use 4 cups of broken up corn bread, 4 slices of fried bacon, cut into small pieces, 1/2 cup of chopped onions, 1/2 cup of diced celery stalks, 1 tablespoonful of herbs (prepared poultry seasoning). Add 1/2 teaspoonful of salt and 1/4 teaspoonful of pepper. Moisten the dressing with giblet stock to which has been added 1 well beaten egg. Finally add 3 tablespoonsful of melted butter. Roast 30 minutes at 350° and 20 minutes to the pound thereafter. It will take at least 2 hours or more to roast the bird.

SIERRA NEVADA CREAM

Beat 3 egg yolks together until light, then add 2 tablespoonsful of cream and beat some more, then add 2 tablespoonsful of (powdered) sugar. Into a pan set into boiling water (double boiler) put 2 cups of heavy cream and 3 bitter almonds and bring to boiling point. Remove the almonds, add the egg mixture and stir constantly until it becomes thickened. Then put into serving dishes.

Shoo Fly Inn at Nortonville

SHOO FLY INN

Mary Ellen, because of her investment with Bell in the black Diamond Coal Company at Nortonville, financially backed the Shoo Fly Inn there.

SHOO FLY PIE

Dissolve 1 teaspoonful of soda in 1 cup of boiling water. Add 1/2 cup of molasses. Then sift into the mixture 1 1/2 cups of flour, 1/2 cup of sugar and add 2 tablespoonsful of melted butter. Line a pie plate with rich pastry (see patty shells page 25). Fill with molasses mixture. Sprinkle on the top the following: 2 tablespoonsful of sugar, 2 tablespoonsful of flour, 2 tablespoonsful of butter mixed together with 1/2 ground nutmeg until topping is creamy. Bake until crust is golden brown 350°.

TYCOON'S BOARDING HOUSE TABLE

Fred Woodworth died in 1865. His home was sold to Milton S. Latham, who was at the crest of a brilliant and eventful career. He had been governor of California and then United States Senator at the age of thirty-three. At the time that he asked Mammy to stay on as his housekeeper he was President of the London and San Francisco Bank.

Additions were made to the house to become a residence of twenty-four rooms, surrounded by a magnificent garden. It soon became the most palatial mansion in California. Mrs. Latham was an invalid and Mary Ellen had little to do. She therefore carried out a plan she had long had in mind. On Washington Street she opened two boarding houses, the one to be patronized by wealthy leading men and the other for clerks working in the Stock Exchange and banks. In this way she kept close track of financial ventures and she and Thomas Bell thereby increased their fortunes.

The place at 920 Washington Street was palatial, the fare tempting to the true gourmet.

Mammy's Elegant Boarding House
at 920 Washington Street, San Francisco

TYCOON'S BOARDING HOUSE

CRAB IN SAUCE

Thoroughly chill the meat from one crab. Into 1/2 cup of olive oil put 1 tablespoonful of capers and 1 tablespoonful of chopped up anchovies. Add 1 teaspoonful of parsley, 1 small green onion chopped up, 1/2 teaspoonful of dry mustard and 1 tablespoonful of white vinegar. Put the crab meat down into the dressing and serve in the crab shells. Decorate with thin slices of hard boiled egg.

SALMON WITH FENNEL SAUCE

Place the salmon in an uncovered bake dish. Sprinkle with salt and pepper and diced onion. Then pour melted butter over it. Bake until a golden brown for 40 or 45 minutes (at 350°). Meanwhile prepare the sauce. First the fresh fennel—a heaping handful—must be very well washed and then put into salted cold water. Drain and tear off the tiny sprigs from the stalks. Put these in a saucepan with 1/2 teaspoonful of salt and 1/8 teaspoonful of soda. Put just enough cold water on the fennel sprigs to cover them. Leave over heat until the water comes to a boil. Then strain off, letting the fennel dry, and chop it up fine. Add to melted butter, sufficient to cover the fish, and let the fennel simmer in the butter for a few minutes. Then pour over the baked fish after the skin has been removed.

LOBSTER IN CURRY SAUCE

Boil 3 lobsters and then cut up the meat. Mix 2 tablespoonsful of softened butter with 2 tablespoonsful of flour. Add 1/2 pint of meat or chicken stock and some salt. Put over heat and stir until thickened. Add 1/2 pint of cream and 1 teaspoonful of curry powder. When smooth, add the cut up lobster and simmer for 5 minutes.

TYCOON'S BOARDING HOUSE

LOUISIANA GUMBO

Cut up a large chicken but not one which is called a stewing fowl. Add to this cut-up lean beef the same weight as the chicken. Brown a large onion in butter at the bottom of a pot. Then put in the chicken parts and meat sections and cover with boiling water. Cook covered until both are tender. Add 100 oysters. They will cook in 15 minutes. Strain off the liquor. Put over heat, adding salt and pepper. Then thicken with pulverized sassafras leaves. Return liquor to stew and serve. (Serves Eight)

VEGETABLES, SERVED COLD

Soak 1 pound of string beans overnight. Cook until tender with 1 onion, 3 tablespoonsful of olive oil, 2 tablespoonsful of vinegar, adding 1 teaspoonful of salt and 1/2 teaspoonful of pepper to the water. Meantime steam 4 small squashes in a colander, placed over a kettle of boiling water. Be careful not to break them when finished. Just before removing the string beans from the fire add 1 cup of cooked garbanzo beans to the boiling water. Drain and remove onion. Put the vegetables on a platter and chill. Serve with the following dressing: Mix together 2 1/2 tablespoonsful of vinegar, 1/2 teaspoonful of lemon juice, 1 teaspoonful of sugar, 1 teaspoonful of salt, 1 teaspoonful of dry mustard (also add 1/4 teaspoonful of paprika). Let stand and when ready to serve fold into the dressing 1 cup of sour cream.

EGGPLANT SAUTE

Select medium-sized eggplants and cut them into slices 1/2 inch thick. Peel each slice. Put the slices into salt water for one hour. Drain and dip each slice in beaten egg to which cream has been added. Then dip into flour and fry in a skillet until slices are nicely brown, using enough grease to cover the bottom of the pan.

TYCOON'S BOARDING HOUSE

BANANA FRITTERS

Sift 2 cups of flour with 3 teaspoonsful of baking powder and 1/2 teaspoonful of salt. Add to the flour mixture 1 beaten egg and 2/3 cup of milk. Strain 2 bananas through a sieve until you have a pulp. Mix with other ingredients. Add 1/4 teaspoonful of lemon juice. Drop by tablespoonsful in boiling shortening, remove when brown and drain on cloth (or paper). Serve with sweetened whipped cream sprinkled with cocoa.

CREPES SUZETTE

Put into a bowl 1/2 pound of flour of a fine grade. Dig a hole into the center of the flour. Into this put a teaspoonful of sugar and 1/8 teaspoonful of salt. Then add 3 eggs, one at a time. Pour into the hole a glass of rum. Mix thoroughly until it is very smooth, adding a little lukewarm water if the batter remains too thick. It should be no thicker than cream. Set aside while making the sauce. Work butter, sugar and the juice of an orange together and melt over a spirit lamp in a silver dish. In a frying pan place a small amount of butter and melt. Then pour 1 tablespoonful of the batter into the pan letting it spread to the edges. As it cooks toss over just once. When the pancake is nicely brown on both sides transfer to the heated sauce. Pour a glassful of curacao over the pancake and set the liquor aflame. Fold over pancake and serve.

PECAN TARTS

Boil together 1 cup of brown sugar and 1/2 cup of hot water. Set it aside to cool. Next beat 2 eggs lightly. Add to the eggs 2 1/2 tablespoonsful of flour and 1/2 teaspoonful of salt. Add 1 cup of milk and cook over hot water (in double boiler) until it is thick and smooth, stirring constantly. When done, add 1/2 of the brown sugar syrup, 1 tablespoonful of butter and 1 teaspoonful of vanilla. Cool mixture. Put into cooked tart shells (see page 25) and place pecans on top, using the remaining syrup to cover the pecans. Chill before serving.

CREME DE MENTHE DESSERT

Whip 1 cup of whipping cream, adding 1/4 cup of powdered sugar and 1/2 teaspoonful of salt. Beat the white of 1 egg until it is stiff enough to stand in peaks and fold into the whipped cream. Add 2 cups of pulverized meringue shells and 6 teaspoonsful of green Creme de Menthe. Pour into molds and cover with a cloth. Do not unmold until ready to serve.

CLOTTED CREAM FOR STRAWBERRIES

Mix together a pint of extra rich milk with a wine glass of rose water and 4 ounces of (powdered) sugar. Add to the liquid the beaten yolks of 2 eggs. Stir this mixture into a quart of best cream and put over hot water (in a double boiler). Let come to a boil while constantly stirring. Let it get cold before serving with strawberries.

Mammy's Boarding House at 520 Washington Street

MAMMY'S OTHER HOUSE

At Mary Ellen's second boarding house, located in the financial district, her Negro waiters gathered for her information on investments. The fare was simple but nourishing.

MAMMY'S OTHER HOUSE

CRISP SPARERIBS

Put 4 pounds of spareribs in a roasting pan, cutting the ribs into sections after they have been split down the middle. This will insure evener cooking and make them easier to serve. Over the ribs place thin slices of lemon and slices of a large onion. When ribs begin to brown baste with the following sauce: To 2 cups of water add 1 cup of catchup, 2 table-spoonsful of Worcestershire sauce, 1 teaspoonful of salt. (Also add 1 teaspoonful of chili powder and 2 drops of tabasco sauce).

AMERICAN POT ROAST

Select a 5 pound chuck roast. Brown 2 sliced onions (also 2 cloves of garlic) in a little suet. Add the meat and sear on all sides down in an iron kettle. Over the meat spread 1 teaspoonful of salt and 1/8 tea-spoonful of pepper. Add 1/2 cup of raisins and 1 bay leaf. Pour over the whole 1 cup of boiling water. Bring water on meat to a boil and then simmer for 2 hours. When meat is finished strain out onions and bay leaf (and garlic) and thicken sauce before pour-ing over meat.

MAMMY'S OTHER HOUSE

BRAISED OXTAIL

Cut off excess fat from 3 large, well-meated, cut-up oxtails. Braise sections until browned in a heavy iron pot. Pour off the excess fat. Add 2 cups of boiling water, a cup of Burgundy wine, salt and pepper and simmer for 3 hours. Serve this dish also with thick noodles. (See page 54)

BEEF SHANK, BOARDING HOUSE STYLE

Cut 3 pounds of young, well-meated, beef shank into cubes. Salt and pepper and dredge with flour. Heat a large iron skillet and brown the beef in a small amount of fat. Add 1 tablespoonful of chopped onion, the shank bones and enough boiling water barely to cover. Add 1/2 cup of already cooked tomatoes, cover tightly, and simmer until tender. Chill and spoon off excess fat from the top. Then remove the bones and add home made noodles (see page 54) which have been cooked separately. (Commercially prepared noodles ruin the dish and should be avoided.)

STUFFED PORK CUTLETS

Lay out 12 pork cutlets. Brown 2 small onions in 4 tablespoonsful of butter. Add 1/2 cup of bread crumbs, some salt and pepper. Bind with beaten egg and a little water. Place some filling on each cutlet, roll and fasten. Place down into deep dish in 1/2 cup of boiling hot water mixed with tomato (1/2 cup of tomato paste.) Bake (at 400°) for 1/2 hour.

MAMMY'S OTHER HOUSE

CHEAP JOHN RUTABAGA

Cook 4 medium sized rutabagas in meat stock to which has been added 3 slices of bacon and 6 allspices, together with 1/2 teasponful of salt and 1/4 teaspoonful of pepper. When the rutabagas begin to soften add 5 pared potatoes and 1/2 teaspoonful of sugar. When the vegetables are both soft mash them, adding 3 tablespoonsful of butter and 1/2 cup of cream. Remove to a deep dish and put buttered crumbs on top and brown in oven.

SOUR-SWEET BEETS

Stir into 1/2 cup of sugar 1 tablespoonful of cornstarch. Mix in 1/2 cupful of vinegar. Stir together and cook over a low fire (double boiler) until the sauce is smooth and thick. Add 12 small beets (precooked) and a sprinkling of caraway seeds. Simmer another 15 minutes, then add 1 tablespoonful of butter.

FRENCH LAMB

Cut the meat from lamb necks to the amount of 4 pounds. Roll each piece in flour to which has been added salt and pepper. Brown in the fat from rendered bacon. Add 1 1/2 cups of already stewed tomatoes. (Also add garlic seasoning). Simmer for 1 hour and then add 6 potatoes cut each into quarters. Just before serving add 1/2 cup of already cooked peas and a little dried parsley.

QUEEN OF HEARTS COOKIES

To 2 cups of sugar add 1 cup of soft butter. Mix into the combination 3 cups of flour, 2 egg yolks and 1 egg white. When smooth roll out the dough until it is thin. Cut with heart-shaped cutter. Beat the remaining egg white and spread on the tops of the cookies. Then sprinkle them with sugar, cinnamon and shaved almonds. Bake at 350° for 10 minutes or until edges are lightly browned.

*Entryway of Mammy's Boarding House
at 520 Washington Street, San Francisco,
as it looked in her time.*

MAMMY'S OTHER HOUSE

LAZY DAY PUDDING

Wash 1 cup of white raisins. Put them down into boiling water and let soak for 1 hour. Then cook for 1/2 hour in the same water. Wash 1/2 cup of rice, add 1 quart of milk and place over boiling water (in double boiler.) Cook until rice is done stirring frequently. Remove from fire, add 2 tablespoonsful of sugar, 1 teaspoonful of vanilla, the raisins and 1/2 teaspoonful of mace. Serve warm.

EARTHQUAKE PUDDING

Cut up into cubes 3 medium slices of white bread. Dot with 2 tablespoonsful of butter and strew with 1/2 cup of white raisins and 1/4 cup of candied citron. Beat 3 eggs. Stir in 1/2 cup of sugar, 2 1/2 cups of milk, 1/2 teaspoonful of vanilla, 1/2 teaspoonful of nutmeg and 1/2 teaspoonful of salt. Pour mixture over cubed bread. Bake for 45 minutes in a moderate oven (350°).

NEW YEAR'S SUPPER

Milton Latham's House

NEW YEAR'S SUPPER

Due to his wife's continued illness Milton Latham preferred to entertain his business friends at noon dinners at Mary Ellen's elegant boarding house. In order to bring Mrs. Latham out of her depressed state the ex-Senator decided to give a great New Year's Day reception with a lavish supper. The glutinous material used to make aspics and molded dishes came from boiling pigs feet and veal knuckle. Such a feast called for oysters, terrapin, sole, roast turkey and stuffed birds served buffet style from tables set with treasures of china, glass and silver. There was a punch bowl filled with appropriate liquid, champagne, and five kinds of wine.

NEW YEAR'S SUPPER

CANVAS BACK DUCKS

Wild ducks must be first parboiled with a large carrot placed in the birds to draw out the fishy taste. Bake at 350° 25 minutes to the pound, placing pork fat over the breasts of the birds and wrapping them in paper which has been greased with fat.

STUFFING FOR DUCKS

For 2 ducks use 1/2 pound of onions. Render out small pieces of pork fat and brown the onions in the fat. To this add 2 pounds of chestnuts from which outer and inside skins have been removed. Together with salt and pepper and 4 tablespoonsful of melted butter cook the chestnuts very slowly until they form a pulp. Stir well and stuff the birds with this.

BAKED TAHOE TROUT

Clean trout, remove heads. Dip the fish in a mixture of beaten egg mixed with heavy cream. Roll well in flour. Lay fish in shallow pan. Sprinkle with salt and pepper and lay strips of bacon lengthwise on the trout and bake until flour coating is well browned.

BAKED HAM, STUFFED

(Prepare ham as described on page 69). Remove the ham bone from the meat. To make the stuffing use finely cut stale bread, peeled chestnuts, an apple sliced (Roman Beauty), melted butter, chopped-up celery and very small pieces of salt pork. Season with 1/8 teaspoonful of thyme, only a pinch of sage, and 1/8 teaspoonful of paprika. Add 1 beaten egg and mix with enough water to moisten the dressing.

MOLDED CUCUMBERS

Slice cucumbers and put into salted water. Heat 3 cups of water to the boiling point and remove from heat. Put into the water 1 blade of mace, 1 teaspoonful of peppercorns and 1/2 bay leaf. Let stand for 15 minutes. Put 6 tablespoonsful of gelatine in 1 cupful of water to dissolve. Strain off mace, peppercorns and bayleaf, add liquid to gelatine and stir to dissolve. Add 1 cup of tarragon vinegar and several drops of green coloring. Rinse mold with cold water and pour enough of the gelatine into the mold to cover the bottom to a depth of 1 inch. When this has set, drain the cucumbers, arrange in a layer in mold, pour the rest of the gelatine into the mold and let jell until firm before serving.

NEW YEAR'S SUPPER

STUFFED EGGPLANT

Cut 2 eggplants in halves. Remove seeded center parts. Then carefully ream out the eggplants leaving only enough in their interiors to retain the shapes of the skins. Boil the seedless portions and mash into a pulp after first draining. Have ready 1 pound of cooked, cleaned shrimp. Dice the shrimp and set aside. Next chop up 2 small onions, 1/2 clove of garlic, 1/2 of a green pepper. Melt 2 tablespoonsful of butter and lightly brown in the butter the onions, garlic and green pepper. Remove from heat and mix with the eggplant pulp and the chopped shrimp. Add salt, pepper and minced parsley. Fill the eggplant skins with the mixture. Spread breadcrumbs over the mixture, pour over them a little melted butter and bake 15 minutes at 350° until the bread crumbs have browned.

BAKED HAM WITH BAR-LE-DUC SAUCE

(Prepare ham as described on page 69). Crush and strain 2 pounds of fresh currants with 1 pound of fresh raspberries. Weigh the resultant pulp. For each pound of pulp add 3/4 pound of sugar. Put on stove, bring to a boil and then cook for 40 minutes over the lowest heat. If it has not jelled in that time cook longer. Then remove from heat and put into crocks and seal the crocks the next day. (The Bar-le-duc sauce can also be used with smoked tongue).

NEW YEAR'S SUPPER

PINK ISLAND PUDDING

Put 2 tablespoonful of gelatine in a bowl. Heat 1 cup of water to boiling, pour over gelatine and stir until gelatine dissolves. Let cool and put into mixture 1 cup of grenadine syrup. Beat the whites of 2 eggs until stiff peaks form. Add to fruit juice and stir well. Rinse out mold with cold water, put in mixture and set in cold place until pudding is firm. Serve with Bavarian Cream.

BAVARIAN CREAM

Soak 2 tablespoonful of gelatin in 1/2 cup of cold water. Add a scalded pint of milk to 4 beaten egg yolks. Then add 1/2 cup of sugar and 1/4 teaspoonful of salt. Cook (in double boiler) until the custard will stick to a spoon, then add the gelatin and stir until dissolved. Add vanilla.

DELIGHT PUDDING

Mix 2 cupsful of milk with 3/4 cup of sugar and 1 teaspoonful of salt and place over hot water (in double boiler). Stir into 1/2 cup of cold milk 4 tablespoonful of cornstarch. Add to mixture of hot milk and stir until thick. Then cover and cook 15 minutes longer. Then slowly add 2 well beaten eggs. Remove from heat, pour into individual molds and chill. Serve with hot butterscotch sauce.

HOT BUTTERSCOTCH SAUCE

Cream 2 level tablespoonful of butter with 1 cup of brown sugar, 1 cup of white sugar and 1/2 teaspoonful of salt. Stir in 1/2 cupful of milk, cook over hot water (in double boiler) and stir mixture until blended and thick. Pour over pudding and decorate with pistachio nuts.

EXOTIC DESSERTS

The Kitchen in Milton Latham's House

EXOTIC DESSERTS

In 1870 Milton Latham married again and although Mammy presided over the household for another three years, during which period lavish parties were given, her schemes for the increase of her wealth had begun to take on gigantic proportions. She decided she had accomplished her desire to know the most influential men of the State. She planned the menu for the last party to be given under her charge at the Latham house, where the mirrors reflected the greatest people of the period.

A caterer had to be called in in order to serve the more than eight hundred guests. Mammy was called upon only to oversee the preparation of some of her most popular desserts and to this end she provided the Negro cooks from her boarding houses to prepare them. (The desserts are reduced to family size).

EXOTIC DESSERTS

SENATOR'S PUDDING

The pudding is very large and 2 cups of water should be used for every 3 ounces of gelatine. Use 8 cups of water and 12 ounces of lemon-flavored gelatine for the size of the pudding given here. Dip the mold in ice water first then fill the mold with the gelatine to a depth of 1 inch. As soon as the jelly has set make a design upon it with 1 pound of fruits that have been preserved in heavy syrup and seasoned with 2 drops of mustard oil. Use: apricots, pears, cherries (light), tangerines, figs, citron, plums, and peaches, and 8 whole almonds. Pour gelatine over the fruits until they are covered by the liquid. Let the jelly on the fruits set. Next set down in the center of the fruit layer another small mold of a 2 cup size. Fill this smaller mold with ice water. Around it pour the rest of the gelatine until it comes to the top of the larger mold. When the whole pudding is firm lift out of the smaller mold and fill the cavity with Bavarian cream. The latter is a soft custard (see page 116) to which sweetened whipped cream, flavored with rum, may be added.

TRANSCENDENT PIE

Beat the yolks of 4 eggs until light and then add 1 1/2 cups of sugar to the yolks. Then beat the whites of the 4 eggs until stiff and add to the yolks. Next stir in 2 teaspoonsful of mixed spices, add 1 cup of blackberry jelly (wild blackberry, if possible), and 1 cup of sweet milk. Line a pie plate with rich pastry, (see patty shells, page 25), pour in mixture and bake until it is firm.

GREENGAGE SHERBET

Use 12 greengage plums (canned). Remove stones and then press fruit through a coarse strainer. Add to the pulp 1/4 cup of sugar (powdered), stirring well and add a little salt. Mix into the mixture 1/2 cup of the juice from the (canned) plums. Then add 1/2 cup of Stewart's Syrup (corn syrup). Blend thoroughly and let stand for a time. Then add 1 cup of heavy cream, pouring it in in a thin stream while gently stirring. Freeze.

EXOTIC DESSERTS

GREENGAGE PASTRY

Make a rich pastry. (See patty shells, page 25.) Place the crust in the bottom of a deep baking dish. Coat the pastry with egg white, then place over it a layer of apricot jam. Fill the dish with peeled, pitted greengage plums that have been halved, sprinkling the layers thickly with sugar, testing to see if the sugar is sufficient. Finally cover the fruit with a round of pastry. Bake at first in hot oven for 10 minutes (at 400°). Then reduce heat and bake 40 minutes longer (at 350°).

STOCK EXCHANGE CUSTARD

Beat 4 eggs lightly. Stir in 1/2 cup sugar and 1/4 teaspoonful of salt. Gradually add 1 quart of scalded milk and then stir vigorously. Place 1 tablespoonful of Vermont maple syrup in the bottom of each custard baking cup. Fill each cup slowly and carefully with the milk and egg mixture by holding a spoon over the syrup and gradually letting the liquid spill out over the edges of the spoon. In this way the syrup will remain at the bottom. Place the custard cups in a pan of hot water and bake in a moderate oven (at 350°) from 35 to 40 minutes or until a knife inserted into the custard comes out clean. Before removing custards chill. Then loosen the edges of the custards with a sharp knife. The syrup will spread over and around the molded custard.

GOLD CREAM

Cook 2 tablespoonsful of tapioca (minute tapioca may be used) in 2 cups of preheated milk over hot water (in a double boiler). Cook until the tapioca is clear, stirring every so often. Combine 1 slightly beaten egg yolk with 1/4 cup of sugar and 1/8 teaspoonful of salt. Pour a small amount of tapioca mixture over egg and sugar combination, return to heat and cook until thickened. Remove from fire and add 3/4 cup of cocoanut. Cool, then fold in the stiffly beaten white of the egg and 1/2 teaspoonful of vanilla.

GENEVA COTTAGE COUNTRY COOKING

GENEVA COTTAGE

Thomas Bell was in the process of building a mansion on Bush Street when the Bank of California crashed, ruining many of the wealthiest men of California. Bell and Mary Ellen knew in advance what was to happen and escaped the disaster. Mrs. Pleasant feared making enemies if this became known. She retired for a long vacation at Geneva Cottage. But in order to convince everyone she had met reverses she raised produce and took a stall in the Washington Market where she sold produce once a week. She took with her to Geneva Cottage one of her boarders from 920 Washington Street and was soon joined by her white protege, Teresa Percy, who was to shortly become Mrs. Bell. Mammy spent a great deal of her time cooking. During this period she received the favorite recipes of her Italian neighbors. She was hoping that Thomas Bell would invite her to become his housekeeper but she was uncertain as to just what she would do in the future.

The Washington Market
as it appeared
in the San Francisco Directory, 1854

GENEVA COTTAGE

ELEGANT FRIED CHICKEN

Cut up a tender frying chicken. Put down into a bowl and pour over it the following mixture: 1 cup salad oil, juice from 1 lemon, 1 teaspoonful of salt, 1/8 teaspoonful of pepper, 1 tablespoonful of chopped fresh parsley and 1 tablespoonful of Worcestershire sauce. Let the chicken soak in this for 2 hours. Then drain thoroughly, dip the chicken parts in rich milk, roll in flour and saute in hot fat for about 20 minutes, frying slowly at first and then briskly when it is almost done.

SHALLOT SAUCE FOR FRIED CHICKEN

Put 1 tablespoonful of cut-up shallots and 1 tablespoonful of cut-up chives in 1/2 cup of white wine. Add a little pepper and 1 tablespoonful of bouillon. Boil down the liquid to about 3 tablespoonsful.

GENEVA COTTAGE

COUNTRY VEAL

Cut 3 pounds of veal tenderloin into strips 2 or 3 inches long. Into a Dutch oven place 3 tablespoonsful of butter, let it melt on top of stove and cook 4 tablespoonsful of minced onions in the butter until they become transparent. Brown the veal strips in the butter. Add 2 cups of chicken broth, 1/4 cup of white wine, 1/2 teaspoonful of rosemary, salt and pepper and pour over veal. Cook until meat is tender in oven (at 350°) being careful not to overcook. About 1 hour is sufficient. Before serving add 1 1/2 teaspoonsful of paprika and a half cup of mushrooms which have been previously cooked.

SOUTHERN PILAU

Using a whole chicken which is young, put it down into a stewing kettle. Lay slices of bacon on the breast and secure in place. Place sliced onions over and around the fowl—2 large onions should be sufficient. Cover the whole with a pint of well washed rice. Then add enough boiling water to cover. Keep the pan tightly closed during the time it takes to cook the fowl, except to remove the cover at the beginning after the water has begun to boil. At that time add salt, pepper, and 1/4 teaspoonful of summer savory. Then reduce heat to simmer until finished.

GENEVA COTTAGE

SUNDAY DINNER PORK

Select 6 meaty rib pork chops. Trim off fat from edges and remove bones. Beat 1 egg and add 1 tablespoonful of cream. Dip pork chops in egg mixture and roll in bread crumbs. Brown the chops in a hot skillet in enough grease to prevent burning. Place the pieces of meat in a bake dish and sprinkle with salt, pepper, and a little poultry seasoning. Put small, tart apples about the sides of the bake dish after having first simmered them in a cup of vinegar mixed with half a cup of water and 1/2 ounce of red cinnamon candy drops. Bake in moderate oven (at 350°) for about 40 minutes, until chops are tender.

FRITTERS TO SERVE WITH ROAST PORK

Mash a cake of yeast down into a cup containing water (1/2 cup). Mix 2 cups of flour with 1/2 teaspoon of salt. Add 1 beaten egg, 1/2 cup of white raisins mixed with currants. Add a tart apple finely chopped and a tablespoonful of candied ginger. Finally add the yeast together with 2 teaspoonsful of lemon juice. Let the dough rise until it is light. Then drop by spoonsful into deep boiling fat and cook until light brown. Upon removing sprinkle the fritters with a mixture of powdered sugar and cocoa.

GENEVA COTTAGE

STUFFED ARTICHOKES, ITALIAN STYLE

Wash 6 artichokes and remove the small, tough outer leaves. Cut off the thorns from remaining leaves. Parboil the artichokes for 10 minutes. Drain and then carefully remove the thin chokes and thistles from the centers. Put in stuffing, made as follows: Mix 1/2 pound of ground-up chuck steak, 1 cupful of dried bread crumbs, 1 clove of finely chopped garlic, 2 well-beaten eggs, 3 tablespoonsful of grated Romano cheese, 1 teaspoonful of chopped parsley or basilico and salt and pepper. Place the stuffed artichokes in a casserole with 1/3 cup of olive oil and 1/4 cup water. Cover tightly and bake in a moderate oven until tender. Serve with spaghetti sauce.

ITALIAN FARMERS' SPAGHETTI SAUCE

Fry 2 ounces of salt pork very slowly so it will not burn and add a little olive oil. Add 1/2 pound of ground up beef. Fry in the fat until the meat loses its red color. Add leaves of mountain mint. Add a clove of garlic and 3 1/2 cups of strained tomatoes. Add 2 bay leaves and salt and pepper. Cook very slowly, keeping the dish covered to preserve flavor. After 1/2 hour add 1 tablespoonful of Romano-pecorino cheese and cook 15 minutes longer.

MOCK BIRDS

Select 2 pounds of veal cut into cutlets at least 1/2 inch thick. Pound the veal cutlets on each side to tenderize. Mix together 1 minced clove of garlic, 1/4 teaspoonful of dried thyme, 1 tablespoonful of lemon juice, salt and pepper, 1 beaten egg yolk and 1/2 cup of beef broth. Break up four slices of bread and pour the mixture over it. Spread the filling out over the veal cutlets, putting a slice of onion in each center. Tie into rolls and secure bacon about them. Bake in a moderate oven (350°) with more beef broth in the bottom of the pan and keep turning them as they cook until they are nicely brown. When ready to serve put sour cream into the liquor left in the pan, and place about the veal birds.

Beltane, the Ranch house in Sonoma,
was designed and built by Mammy
and still stands intact.

GENEVA COTTAGE

JAMBALAYAH

Use 1 cup of diced cooked chicken and 1 cup of diced cooked veal and 1 cup of already boiled rice. Add 1 chopped-up onion, 1 green pepper, 1 large stalk of celery minced. Pour over the whole 1 1/2 cups of already stewed tomatoes and heat on top of the stove. If the seasoning of the leftovers is sufficient, salt and pepper need not be added. When heated place the mixture in a bake dish and cover with buttered crumbs and brown in the oven. A 1/2 teaspoonful of marjoram may be used as seasoning if desired.

'49er LAMB

Have 2 lamb breasts cut up into 2 inch long pieces. Remove surplus fat. Then drop the meat into boiling water. Put in 1 teaspoonful of salt and 1 tea-spoonful of allspice. When meat is tender remove from the liquid and take out the bones. Place the meat in a bake dish and place over it 6 medium sized potatoes, sliced thin. Sprinkle 2 chopped onions over the whole. Thicken the liquor from off the meat, add 1 sliced pickled cucumber. Pour this over the mixture reserving at least 2 cupsful of the liquor. When the dish is finished add 1/2 glass of currant jelly to the remaining liquor and pour this over the whole.

LOQUAT JELLY

Clean the fruit of ends. Place in cold water to cover and put over fire cooking slowly until the fruit is so soft that the juice is freed. Strain the juice and cook it down until it becomes cherry colored. It is then thick enough to add sugar to taste and boil again until the sugar dissolves and the jelly forms.

GENEVA COTTAGE

RASPBERRY JOY

To 1 pint of fresh raspberries add 1/2 cup of cold water and 1/2 cupful of sugar. Cook until they are very soft and then press them through a fine seive to remove the seeds. Reheat the juice and when it has reached the boiling point add 2 tablespoonsful of tapioca (quick cooking) 2 teaspoonsful of salt and 1 tablespoon of lemon juice. Cook over hot water (in double boiler) until the tapioca becomes transparent. Serve with sweetened whipped cream.

BUTTERSCOTCH PIE

Heat 1/2 cup of water with 2 cups of brown sugar. Bring to boiling point. Quickly remove from stove and pour sugared water over the following mixture: 2 tablespoonsful of flour, 2 tablespoonsful of cornstarch and some salt. Then gradually add 1 1/2 cups of cream. When the mixture has become thick add 3 large, well-beaten eggs. Cook for 1 minute, remove from fire, add 1/8 pound of butter and some vanilla. Turn into an already baked pastry shell. (see page 25). Cover with sweetened whipped cream.

GOLDEN FRUIT PUDDING

Cut up fresh peaches to the amount of 2 cups. Add to them 1/2 cup of sugar. Put down into baking dish. Then mix together 1/4 cup of flour, 2 teaspoonsful of baking powder and 3/4 cup of milk and stir until smooth. Pour the batter over the peaches. Melt 2 tablespoonsful of butter and pour over the batter. Bake for 1 hour (at 350°.)

GENEVA COTTAGE

APRICOT PIE

Press 3 cups of cooked apricots through a sieve. Mix 2/3 cup of sugar, 1/8 teaspoonful of salt and 3 tablespoonsful of cornstarch. Blend this mixture with the apricot pulp and cook over hot water (in double boiler) for about 15 minutes. Remove from fire and add 2 tablespoonsful of butter and 2 tablespoonsful of lemon juice. Cool before putting in precooked rich pastry shell (see page 25). Cover with sweetened whipped cream.

BLACKBERRY FLUFF

Melt a 6 ounce glass of blackberry jelly over hot water (in double boiler). When it is melted pour it slowly over the stiffly beaten whites of 3 eggs and beat until well blended (with rotary beater). Finally fold in 1/3 cup of chopped walnut meats. Turn the whole into a well buttered baking dish and bake for 25 minutes (at 375°) or until a knife when inserted into the dessert comes out clean. Serve with liquid custard. (See page 45.)

*This House at 2016 Pine Street,   San Francisco, was
Designed and Built by Mammy for a Favorite Protege,
Rebecca Howard Gordon*

133

GENEVA COTTAGE

COUNTRY AFTERNOON TEA COOKIES

Melt 1 1/2 cups of butter and pour over it 1 1/2 cups of sugar. Add 1 whole egg and 1 egg yolk and beat the mixture until it becomes foamy. Sift flour and measure out 2 1/2 cups. Stir into the flour 1 cup of finely ground almonds. Add 1/2 teaspoonful of ground cardamon seed and 1 tablespoonful of orange juice. Put the two mixtures together and beat. First chill the dough and then roll out very thin and cut into crescent shapes. Bake (at 375°) for 10 minutes.

COWSLIP WINE

Measure out the heads of cowslips until a 4 quart container is filled, selecting the middle of the day to gather them when there is no dew. Squeeze out the juice of 3 oranges and 3 lemons. Pour over cowslips, then cut up the rinds and add them to the flower heads. Place in a crock. Then boil 2 gallons of water with 8 pounds of sugar. If scum forms, remove it. When sugar has melted pour over the flower mixture. Stir very thoroughly with a wooden spoon until it is lukewarm. Dissolve 3 3/4-ounce packages of yeast cake in warm water and pour into the crock. Cover the crock and put it in a warm place for 6 days, stirring once every day. Then strain into gallon jars and let wine ferment. After fermentation has taken place, strain off flowers and peels and decant the cowslip wine into bottles.

ANGELICA WINE

Put 2 gallons of water into an enamel cooking pot. Squeeze the juice out of 2 lemons and 2 oranges and put into the water and add the rinds of both fruits. Crush 1 pound of angelica leaves and add to the mixture. Heat the liquid to boiling point and let boil for 25 minutes. Strain into a crock, again squeezing leaves to get their full flavor. Add 7 pounds of sugar and let it dissolve in the liquid until the latter is lukewarm. Put 1/2 ounce of yeast in 1/2 cup of warm water. Press until dissolved and pour it into the wine mixture. Finally cover the crock and put it in a warm place. Fermentation will take about 2 weeks. Then again strain and rack. It will not be ready for use until a year has gone by.

Los Alamos Ranch House near Santa Barbara

LOS ALAMOS RANCHO

In 1873 Thomas Bell had asked Mammy Pleasant to help him select a ranch. North of Santa Barbara they discovered an old Spanish ranch on the Coast, called Los Alamos. A property of two thousand acres, which included both mountains and valleys, it commanded a magnificent view of the Pacific Ocean. Mammy persuaded her partner to invest his money in the place because it was especially suited "for raising beans." Neither Bell nor his advisor had any suspicion that this land would ultimately cause the oil magnate, Edward L. Doheny, to purchase it for $1,500,000 from Bell's estate.

Bell still did not engage Mary Ellen to be his housekeeper, as she had hoped, when he completed the building of his Bush Street house. Instead, he asked her to design and oversee the building of a large ranch house at Los Alamos. When the house was finished she stayed there for a brief time, trying her hand at preparing vegetables for the table in unusual ways.

LOS ALAMOS RANCHO

SALSIFY SOUP

Scrape the salsify (oyster plant) and chop up enough to measure out 1 cup. Cook in water until soft and then drain. Mash the herb and then add 1 pint of milk. Add 2 1/2 tablespoonsful of butter. Boil for 2 minutes while stirring. Mix 1 tablespoonful of cornstarch with 1/2 cup of milk. Then stir this into the milk and put a blade of mace in at the same time. Carefully cook until the cornstarch has thickened the soup. Remove the mace and add white pepper and salt before serving.

EGG BALLS FOR SOUP

Mash 3 hard boiled eggs into a smooth paste. Add a little melted butter, salt and pepper and thoroughly mix with a raw egg. Form the mixture into small balls and drop into boiling soup 3 minutes before serving.

GREEN TOMATO MINCEMEAT

Use 4 cups of water and 1 cup of vinegar to 1 peck of green tomatoes. Cook slowly for 2 hours. Then add 2 pounds of chopped dark raisins, 3 pounds of white sugar, 1 pound of brown sugar, 2 tablespoonsful of cinnamon, 2 tablespoonsful of nutmeg, 2 tablespoonsful of allspice, and 1/8 teaspoonful of ground cloves. Cook for 2 more hours. Put away in crocks in a cool place for holiday use.

GREEN TOMATOES, RANCHO STYLE

Cut green tomatoes into slices about 1/4 inch thick. Dab slices with a towel to remove any excess moisture. Then dust them with salt and pepper. Beat 1 egg until very light and add a little cream. Dip each slice into this then into bread crumbs. Fry until brown on one side then turn over and fry the other side. Serve with Hollandaise sauce.

Thomas Bell's Bachelor Home at 1107 Bush Street, San Francisco

LOS ALAMOS RANCHO

SWEET GLAZED POTATOES

Select 6 medium potatoes. Wash and pare and cook for 10 minutes in boiling, salted water. Drain and then cut lengthwise in halves. Put in a buttered pan. Boil 1/2 cup of brown sugar with 2 tablespoonsful of water for 3 minutes. Add 4 tablespoonsful of butter and baste until they are tender.

FRANCONIA POTATOES

Select medium size potatoes. Wash and peel and dry very thoroughly. Arrange in a roasting pan with lamb and cook at the same time as the meat, baking and turning the potatoes during the cooking period so they will be evenly browned.

SANTA BARBARA CHILI SAUCE

Measure out 8 quarts of ripe tomatoes and peel them, holding each over a flame to loosen the skin. Add 3 cups of red chiles, chopped, 3 cups of onions, coarsely chopped, 2 cups of sugar, 2 teaspoonsful of salt, and 1 1/2 quarts of vinegar. Season with 3 teaspoonsful of cloves, 3 teaspoonsful of cinnamon, 3 teaspoonsful of nutmeg, 3 teaspoonsful of ginger. Boil for 3 hours. Then it is ready for use.

COAST KOHLRABI

Select 6 kohlrabi. Wash and peel and cut into cubes. Drop into boiling water and cook until tender. Use with a white sauce (see page 10).

LOS ALAMOS RANCHO

FRUITED BEETS

Place 1 dozen thinly sliced, uncooked beets in a baking dish. Mix together 2 tablespoonsful of flour with 1/2 cup of sugar and 1/2 teaspoonful of salt. Then pour 1/2 cup of orange juice over the beets and dot with 2 tablespoonsful of butter. Bake for 60 minutes (at 300°).

CHIFFONADE DRESSING FOR LETTUCE

To 3/4 cup of well-seasoned French dressing add the following: 2 tablespoonsful of minced fresh parsley, 2 tablespoonsful of chopped sweet red pepper, 1 tablespoonful of chopped green onion, 1 chopped-up hard boiled egg, 1/4 cup of cooked beets. Let the mixture stand for several hours before serving.

MAMMY'S HIGHLAND FLING

MAMMY'S HIGHLAND FLING

When Mary Ellen had finished organizing the operation of the Los Alamos ranch she returned to San Francisco. As soon as she returned Bell went to Los Alamos ranch for a long vacation. She still had it in mind that her business partner would wish her to manage his new city mansion. Anticipating this she tried her hand at a few dishes she knew would please Bell, a Scotsman.

The Thomas Bell Mansion at 1661 Octavia Street

MAMMY'S HIGHLAND FLING

SALLY LUNN

Scald 1 cup of milk. Add to it 2 tablespoonsful of shortening, 2 tablespoonsful of sugar, and 1/2 teaspoonful of salt. Let cool to lukewarm. Add a yeast cake softened in 1/4 cup of lukewarm water. Then add 3 well beaten eggs. Finally stir into the entire mixture 3 and 3/4 cups of flour and beat vigorously. Let rise in a warm place until the dough has doubled in bulk which will take about 2 hours. Beat again. Fill greased muffin tins two thirds full. Let rise until again double in bulk. Then bake in a moderate oven (at 350°) until nicely brown.

OAT CAKES

Put 2 cups of oatmeal in a mixing bowl; rub in 1 tablespoonful of shortening, 1/2 teaspoonful of salt, and add enough water to make a stiff dough. Dust the bread board with oatmeal and roll batter out thin. Cut the cake into a round big enough to fit a griddle and slip it carefully onto the hot iron. Just before it begins to cook, cut the round into quarters. Bake (at 300°) until crisp and delicately brown. Then, if the cake is found not to be quite hard enough, it can be returned to the oven until it is thoroughly dried out.

CHRISTMAS CAKE

Mix 3/4 pound of butter with 1 pound of brown sugar. Add 10 beaten eggs. Put 3/4 teaspoonful of soda in a little water and stir in. Then begin to add 5 cups of flour alternately with 3/4 cup of brandy mixed with 1/2 cup of rose water. Finally stir in 2 pounds of currants, 2 pounds of raisins, 1 pound of dates, 1/4 pound of almonds, 1/4 pound of walnuts, 1/2 teaspoonful of cloves, 1 teaspoonful of allspice, 1 teaspoonful of mace, and 1 teaspoonful of mixed spice. Finally add 1 teaspoonful of vanilla. Stir until thoroughly mixed. If the dough is stiff a little more brandy may be added. Bake in well greased, floured bread pans until a straw comes out clean. (At 350°.)

MAMMY'S HIGHLAND FLING

PICAITHLEY SCONES

Sift together 4 cups of flour, 3 teaspoonsful of baking powder and 1/2 teaspoonful of salt. Rub into the mixture 2 tablespoonsful of butter. Then mix to a soft dough with 1 1/2 cups of milk. Turn out on a floured board and roll into rounds. Dust the griddle thinly with flour, slip on the round of dough cut into quarters. Bake slowly (at 275°) and do not turn it over until the top is beginning to show bubbles. Turn only once and serve hot.

TEA SQUARES WITH DATES

Cream 1 cup of butter with 1 cup of sugar. Add 1 cup of flour and 2 1/2 cups of rolled oats and 1/2 teaspoonful of salt. Stir well until the mixture holds together. Divide the dough into 2 halves. Spread the first half on an ungreased baking dish and smooth it out. Then spread the dough in a square baking dish with the following filling: Cook pitted dates with water over low heat until a paste is formed. When cool add a teaspoonful of lemon juice. Then smooth the second half of the dough over the filling. Mark the whole into 2 inch squares. Cook 30 minutes in a medium oven (350°.)

SCOTTISH SCONES WITH RAISINS

Mix together 3 cups of flour with 2 teaspoonsful of baking powder. Cream 1 cup of butter and add 1 cupful of sugar. Then begin to add the flour mixture, alternately with 1/2 cup of milk and 1/2 cup of cream. Finally add 1 cup of chopped raisins. Then stir in the well beaten white of an egg. Roll the dough out until it is about 1/2 inch thick. Cut into triangles and brush with the well beaten yolk of the egg. Bake until nicely brown. (At 350°).

146

Steiner Street House, still standing,
once owned by Teresa Bell

WOMAN
OF
MYSTERY

WOMAN OF MYSTERY

In 1876 Mammy Pleasant built a great mansion on the slope of Holliday's Hill. It had thirty rooms and cost $100,000, an operation that took almost three years to complete because of the elaborate frescoes decorating its interior. Mammy's white protege, Teresa Percy, moved into the house and Thomas Bell married her and came there to live later on. The members of San Francisco society refused to accept Teresa and Mammy's days as a famous cook, presiding over a palatial mansion, came to an end.

Teresa became known as "The Woman of Mystery" and she was a source of excessive curiosity not only in the city but to visitors from such far-away places as London, Paris, and Berlin, where newspapers had described her at some length.

After Mammy's Death, Teresa Bell, her protege,
Moved to this House
on Laidley Street in San Francisco

INDEX

INDEX

INDEX

INDEX

INDEX

Mammy Pleasant died in this house
at 2781 Filbert Street
at the Age of 89 in January of 1904.

157

BIOGRAPHICAL INFORMATION

Helen Holdredge was born in Duluth, Minnesota and comes from a family noted as historians. She attended private schools in Portland and the University of Oregon. Mrs. Holdredge has had successive careers as an illustrator, radio singer, soloist for the Scotch Band of Portland and was for a time in opera. She wrote for a number of years under a pseudonym but emerged as a biographer when *Mammy Pleasant* was published. This was followed by other best sellers: *Mammy Pleasant's Partner*, *The Woman in Black* (Lola Montez) *The House of the Strange Woman* and *Firebelle Lillie* (Lillie Coit). In preparation is another biography, *Love Goddess: Aimee Crocker*.

Mrs. Holdredge is the widow of Claire P. Holdredge, distinguished geologist and explorer.

James Beauchamp Alexander, architect and author, was born at San Francisco. He is a graduate of Washington and Lee University and has degrees from the Royal Academy of Copenhagen and from Ecole Des Beaux Arts at Fontainbleau. He is a veteran of World War II and the Korean campaign and is widely travelled. The author of a history of architecture, he is currently writing a book on San Francisco mansions. Lately he served as Executive Director of the California Heritage Council and is considered to be an authority on San Francisco history.

Mr. Alexander is the descendant of the Price family of Missouri, a member of which, Americus Price, bought Mammy Pleasant and gave her her freedom.

OTHER GOURMET BOOKS FROM 101 PRODUCTIONS

Greek Cooking for the Gods by Eva Zane
Vegetarian Gourmet Cookery by Alan Hooker
101 Secrets of California Chefs by Jacqueline Killeen
101 Nights in California, a Guide with Menus
The Hard Times Cookbook, by Gloria Vollmayer and Carmen Wyllie